Coming Out Queer Online

Lexington Studies in Communication and Storytelling

Series Editors: Kathleen M. Ryan, University of Colorado Boulder
and Deborah A. Macey, University of Washington Tacoma

Lexington Studies in Communication and Storytelling engages scholarship in mediated storytelling, be it the traditional book or television program, the performed oral narrative, or the emerging media platform. Interdisciplinary in scope, this series looks at the myriad theoretical and practical approaches to the story. From the audience member-turned creator to new narrative, this series explores what storytelling means in the twenty-first century.

Recent titles in the series:

Coming Out Queer Online: Identity, Affect, and the Digital Closet, by Patrick M. Johnson
The Audience and Business of YouTube and Online Videos, edited by Louisa Shu Ying Ha
Friends, Lovers, Co-Workers, and Community: Everything I Know about Relationships I Learned from Television, edited by Kathleen M. Ryan and Deborah A. Macey
Mothers Work: Confronting the Mommy Wars, Raising Children, and Working for Social Change, by Michelle Napierski-Prancl

Coming Out Queer Online

Identity, Affect, and the Digital Closet

Patrick M. Johnson

LEXINGTON BOOKS
Lanham • Boulder • New York • London

Published by Lexington Books
An imprint of The Rowman & Littlefield Publishing Group, Inc.
4501 Forbes Boulevard, Suite 200, Lanham, Maryland 20706
www.rowman.com

6 Tinworth Street, London SE11 5AL, United Kingdom

British Library Cataloguing in Publication Information Available

Library of Congress Cataloging-in-Publication Data

Names: Johnson, Patrick M., 1984- author.
Title: Coming out queer online : identity, affect, and the digital closet / Patrick M. Johnson.
Description: Lanham : Lexington Books, [2020] | Series: Lexington studies in communication and storytelling | Includes bibliographical references and index.
Identifiers: LCCN 2020009027 (print) | LCCN 2020009028 (ebook) | ISBN 9781793613462 (cloth) | ISBN 9781793613479 (epub) | ISBN 9781793613486 (pbk)
Subjects: Subjects: LCSH: Sexual minorities. | Coming out (Sexual orientation) | Social media.
Classification: LCC HQ73 .J63 2020 (print) | LCC HQ73 (ebook) | DDC 306.76--dc23
LC record available at https://lccn.loc.gov/2020009027
LC ebook record available at https://lccn.loc.gov/2020009028

I dedicate this work in the memory of Emily Margaret Gould, who passed away on September 5, 2016. Even though she was only on this earth for but a few years, through her smiles and the tireless work of her parents, Meghan and Jim (two of the strongest people I know) she made a lasting impact on everyone who knew her.

I never got to meet Emily in person, but through Facebook I had the ability to develop a deep bond with my cousin. Stories like Emily's showcase the true potential and power that social media have to radically change people's lives and bring people together.

Rest in peace, Emily.

Contents

Acknowledgments

This work would not have been possible without the help from countless individuals who helped me along the way. I hope to pay tribute and express my gratitude to everyone who has helped me with this journey. While I will attempt to make this an exhaustive list, inevitably some people will be left off this list, but know that I am very humbled by the amount of support I have had from many people throughout my life.

I would not have been able to complete this without the helpfulness of all the participants. Thank you, from the bottom of my heart, for being willing to open up and share your amazing and wonderful stories with me. You truly inspired me every day as I was working on this project and continue to do so to this day. Hearing your experiences and your desires for being about good and positive change in this world, not just for LGBT*Q+ individuals, but for everyone, resonated with me deeply. You are all such strong individuals, so thank you for giving me the privilege of getting to capture your experiences and share them with the world.

I cannot overstate the helpfulness of each and every one of my colleagues who supported me throughout this process. Dr. Polly McLean was very helpful through the development of this study and for being supportive through the entire process. She also exposed me to invaluable research and perspectives that were foundational for the theoretical and methodological framework that helped me conceive of this project. Dr. Stewart Hoover also was invaluable throughout my academic progression at the University of Colorado (CU) Boulder, particularly in inspiring me to understand the importance of religion in the creation of norms within the United States. Dr. Kathleen Ryan has been an inspiration and a role model consistently throughout my academic career. She was helpful in numerous respects including expanding my methodological understand of how to understand visuals, how to blend both creative and academic endeavors, and emotional support. Dr. Kwame Holmes helped to provide a fresh perspective on queer theory and encouraged me to expand my thinking into different fields. Through our weekly coffee meetings, he taught me to be a better scholar and how to work together with others to unpack complex readings and apply these ideas to contemporary issues in an interdisciplinary way. Dr. Celeste Montoya inspired me to change the way that I thought about methodology and helped provide me a solid foundation in feminist inquiry and an understanding of the many different types of feminisms that exist.

This project would never have come to fruition without the love and support from my parents, Sam and Diane Johnson. Without their unwavering support and always pushing me to set my goals high, I would not be where I am today. Coming out to one's parents is a scary experience for anyone, and I cannot express enough gratitude for the way my parents have accepted and embraced me for who I am. I also need to thank my brother, Dr. Aaron Johnson, who has inspired me throughout my life and has always been a source of emotional support, a great sounding board, and a role model who I have always looked up to.

My friends have been very supportive throughout this process, particularly Dr. Luis Medina for proofreading and giving advice throughout as well as Dr. Shannon O'Sullivan and Bobbi Newman, who were great sounding boards and served as both role models and friends. Finally, I would be remiss to not acknowledge and thank my boyfriend Rocky Rowley for providing the emotional support needed to get through this project; he has always been a source of encouragement and support.

This work was a collaboration with many talented, smart, ambitious, and admirable individuals, and I cannot express adequately the amount of thanks I feel toward every person who helped me along this journey.

Thank you.

Chapter One

Identity in the Digital Age

Coming out is not an easy or quick process for anyone. Despite representations in media that focus on the first public declaration of one's sexuality as a climactic moment, the truth of coming out is that it happens in phases and cycles and never truly begins or ends. Living in the Lesbian, Gay, Bisexual, Transgender, and Queer (LGBT*Q+)[1] community in our modern social media–driven world is to be living in a continual state of coming out. Every post one makes, meme one shares, or image that one likes is a potential of coming out to a new individual. Before it is even shared with the world, an LGBT*Q+ individual is in a constant state of coming out to oneself—taking in the messages they receive from the world about the LGBT*Q+ community and figuring out where and how they fit in with that. Social media has in some ways fundamentally changed they way people interact and form connections. Despite the medium and form changing, the content and context of messages has remained shockingly stagnant.

The LGBT*Q+ community has always been on the forefront of technology, always using the latest technology to carve out places of belonging, meaning, and social connection. Technology and social media have thus created new forms of safe, inclusive spaces for people to exist outside of the white, cisgender, and heteronormative world that occupies much of society. They have allowed individuals to survive and even thrive, even when living in locations and times that deem their very existence as an existential threat to morality. These same technologies, however, amplify stereotypes and bigotry and, in part, determine access into these spaces. They have also opened up new risks of exposing personal details of one's life to those who rather they did not exist. They have allowed for new divides to occur within the LGBT*Q+ community—or rather strengthened divides that have always been there. For many, social media is not viewed as the real world. It is a place to escape the pressure, the monotony, and the dangers of the real world. For many within the LGBT*Q+ community, social media has formed a new society. Places that allow people to be who they are and who they wish they could be. For some within the LGBT*Q+ community, their online lives are much more authentic and real than the ones they lead within the "real" world. Much like the dangers LGBT*Q+ people face in society, social media can contain all of these same or even more dangers, sometimes leading to tragic results.

This book is the result of two years of interviews, newspaper analysis, and social media analysis. In a way though, it is also the culmination of my life up to this point having grown up as a gay man in a socially conservative city around the dawn of social media. Growing up in the late 1980s and throughout the turn of the century in the small city of Erie, Pennsylvania, the only exposure I had to the LGBT*Q+ community was through news stories about either Pride parades or the ongoing AIDS epidemic. While this provided visibility to this community, it was often in a negative light, which greatly influenced my perceptions on what it meant to be gay in the United States. Coming of age at the end of the twentieth century, I had the experience of growing up with the development of digital technology that paved the way for social media to evolve. In college, I was exposed to my first glimpses of gay-specific social media and LGBT*Q+ individuals. Even though I was not yet "out" to anyone, even to myself, I was able to use social media to connect with gay men both locally and at a distance. I kept this secret from everyone and was hesitant to use other popular social media platforms at the time (e.g., Myspace or Friendster). In my first year of my undergraduate degree, Facebook was first released and quickly took off across colleges, spanning the country as a way to connect with others on campus and keep up with friends from high school.

Growing up in a small, working-class city in northern Pennsylvania in a Roman Catholic household, being LGBT*Q+ was not desirable. Even though most of my family members were not overtly anti-LGBT*Q+, there was an understanding of how difficult life would be for someone who lived life as an LGBT*Q+ individual. Going to an LGBT*Q+-friendly college, having friends who were LGBT*Q+, and interacting with gay and bisexual men online slowly helped to shift my mentality about being gay in the United States. Through chat rooms such as Gay.com, I met and talked with gay individuals who were leading happy and successful lives. Once I moved to Los Angeles after graduating, I started dating men through the assistance of various social media sites, both gay-specific ones and "mainstream"[2] sites, such as Myspace. Through these interactions I could take the first step and come out to myself before eventually coming out to friends and family (only after I had already begun a serious relationship).

During this time of being partially out, posting on social media was a complicated situation. Prior to finishing college, I used Facebook but never used Myspace until I started coming out. This allowed me to craft two very different personas online. One remained the same while the other allowed me the opportunity to explore expression of my new sexual identity. These different sites expressing different identities for me acted as extensions for the way I was already performing my identity in life. One of the reasons I kept these two spaces different was I felt, at the time, that it was inappropriate to come out to friends and family that I had not seen in a while (but followed on Facebook) through social media. When I did decide to post about my relationship online and photos from my first gay pride event, it proved to be a liberating moment for me. Even though I was nervous about going back to my hometown and seeing my family and friends around the holidays, those fears proved to be moot as I did not have to individually come out to anyone, and nobody seemed offended by the fact that they learned about this through social media. It was this experience that made me start to consider the ways that the coming-out experience was changing for LGBT*Q+ individuals throughout the country because of the influence of social media.

EVOLUTIONS OF COMING OUT AND SOCIAL MEDIA

Data from the Pew Research Center (2013) shows that the average lesbian, gay, or bisexual individual begins to realize they are not heterosexual around the ages of ten to thirteen; however, the average person does not come out until approximately ten years later. There are many fears that may contribute to this: bullying, social stigma, rejection from family or friends, the dread of being an outcast in society, or the threat of physical violence. These are not unfounded fears either, even if acceptance of LGBT*Q+ individuals has increased dramatically since the 1960s. More than 50 percent of LGBT*Q+ individuals within the United States have been the subject of homophobic or transphobic slurs, nearly 40 percent of LGBT*Q+ individuals reported having been rejected by family or friends, and 30 percent report having been physically threatened or assaulted (Pew Research Center 2013).

Even though the LGBT*Q+ rights movement is often considered to have started in 1969 during the Stonewall Riots, the decades that followed were a roller coaster ride with certain advances gained along with major setbacks, such as the passing of Don't Ask, Don't Tell (DADT) and the Defense of Marriage Act (DOMA) in the 1990s. After the turn of the century, overall acceptance for the LGBT*Q+ community began to change. This was partly due to a series of court cases, starting in 2003 with *Lawrence v. Texas*, which ruled that a prohibition of sodomy was unconstitutional. This was followed by the repealing of both DADT and DOMA, and it culminated with the lifting of a ban on transgender individuals serving in military in 2016 (CNN 2016), which was reinstated in 2018. There has also been an increase in portrayals of the LGBT*Q+ community on television and movies, even garnering praise at some of the top awards within the industry (Battles and Hilton-Morrow 2002; Becker 2006; Bonds-Raacke et al. 2007; Branson-Potts 2015; Sorren 2015).

Despite an increase in acceptance of the community, many individuals within the LGBT*Q+ community are often the victims of discrimination. One of the main issues facing LGBT*Q+ youth is bullying, both in school and on social media, sometimes ending in physical assault, homicide, and suicide (Carosone 2013; Asala 2010; J. K. Puar 2012; Remafedi, Farrow, and Deisher 1991). Transgender individuals of all ages have faced additional discrimination in the form of "bathroom laws" such as HB2 in North Carolina, which required individuals to use the bathroom consistent with their biological sex, not their gender identity (Gordon and Price 2016). Following the legalization of same-sex marriage, numerous states enacted religious freedom bills, essentially allowing business owners to choose not to offer goods or services to someone based on their gender or sexual identity. The election of Donald Trump and Michael Pence (who, as governor, had written the "religious freedom" bill in Indiana and worked to fund gay conversion therapy) created a culture of fear and uncertainty among many in the LGBT*Q+ community who felt their gender or sexual identity could become criminalized yet again. In the years following the 2018 election and the appointment of Justice Brett Kavanaugh to the US Supreme Court, both a transgender military ban and religious-based LGBT*Q+ discrimination have been upheld by the Supreme Court (Dolan 2019; de Vogue and Cole 2019).

Since the start of the new millennium, technology has been evolving at an ever-increasing rate. In 2016, 90 percent of US adults actively used the Internet, an increase of 70 percent since 2000 (Smith 2017). In an even faster increase, between 2005 and 2016, the amount of US adults who used social media increased by 1,280 percent, from only 5 percent of all US adults to almost 70 percent (Smith 2017). When looking at the breakdown of social media usage among different age-groups, a substantial majority of these individuals are in the eighteen-to-forty-nine-year-old age-group, indicating the substantial role that social media plays within the lives of millennials, Xenials, and Gen Xers (Smith 2017). In 2016 adults in the United States spent an average of five and a half hours on social media each week, with those aged thirty-five to forty-nine spending almost seven hours per week, an increase of almost 30 percent from the previous year (The Nielson Company 2017). Social media has quickly become integral to the way individuals communicate with friends, family, and strangers across the globe. As van Dijck elucidates "connective media have almost become synonymous with sociality; you can check out anytime you 'like,' but you can never leave"

(2013, 175). In other words, in our current media moment it is almost impossible to socialize without facilitation in some way through social media. This has led to the dissolution of the idea of a center of media production with media producers on one side and the audience on the other as two separate entities (Couldry, 2012; Jenkins, 2008; Shaw, 2015; van Dijck, 2013).

Since acceptance of the LGBT*Q+ community and usage of social media have increased simultaneously, it is important to examine the role that an increase in the use of social media has had upon both the acceptance of, and the lives of individuals within, the LGBT*Q+ community. As Pullen notes:

> This offers new opportunities for action and coalescence, allowing for the showcasing of diverse sexuality. The Internet and the World Wide Web *seemingly* reveal a patchwork of new social worlds, offering scope beyond the virtual and the disconnected. Whether this is concerned with identity, representation, production, consumption, or self-regulation, LGBTs are defining new pathways distant from historical confines. (2010, 1)

These emancipatory hopes for social media and the LGBT*Q+ community are relatively common within discourses about how individuals will now be able to interact in completely new ways online, with the idea that these platforms offer spaces that are no longer bounded by the same social mores and norms that once constrained LGBT*Q+ individuals (Craig and McInroy 2014a; Etengoff and Daiute 2015; Pullen and Cooper 2010). As van Dijck points out, "social media constitute an arena of public communication where norms are shaped and rules get contested" (2013, 19). He also goes on to explain that even though norms are shaped and challenged through social media, it is not always because of the interactions of individuals who are able to act autonomously, but that through defaults and platform settings the companies that control the social network are able to control many of these changing social norms (van Dijck 2013). This is an issue that became apparent when Facebook unveiled its "real name policy" in 2014 in a desire that all people should be completely "authentic" and transparent within their social media (Grinberg 2014). Some social media sites desire complete transparency (e.g., Facebook), while others thrive on anonymity (e.g., Twitter, Reddit). Once considered to be a highlight of social media, there have been many incidents where the anonymity online led to increased bullying and negative remarks (Christopherson 2007; Hlavach and Freivogel 2011; Marwick and boyd 2011; Moore et al. 2012).

Many scholars who have researched and theorized about social media tend to fall either on the side of praising its potential (Craig and McInroy 2014a; Jenkins 2008; Pullen and Cooper 2010) or critiquing its harm (Hlavach and Freivogel 2011; Marwick and boyd 2011; Moore et al. 2012). Rather than examining social media along these poles, it is my contention that we need to study social media by focusing on how content, platforms, and networks impact the everyday lives of individuals. In this way, content on social media is not separate from the individuals who create or consume it, but rather an extension of their identity.

Social media is simultaneously shown to provide a voice to underserved and underrepresented populations (Brundidge 2010; Gorkemli 2012; Juris 2012; Marciano 2011; Solomon et al. 2015) and an increased harassment of people already at risk of bullying (Christopherson 2007; Hlavach and Freivogel 2011; Hughey and Daniels 2013; Marwick and boyd 2011; Poole 2013). The potential for empowerment is often based on the ability for individual, rather than group, action, which has been criticized as de-politicizing these spaces (J. Dean 2005). Recent political and social trends within the LGBT*Q+ community have been criticized as reinforcing heteronormativity, whiteness, and cisgender-ness (e.g., the emphasis on same-sex marriage and centering those who are "passing") (Duggan 2002; Halberstam 2005; Muñoz 2009; Jasbir K. Puar 2010; Ross 2005; Wight 2014). Social media, therefore, has the potential for liberation and harm simultaneously, especially given the precarious social position many LGBT*Q+ individuals occupy. There has been a trend in recent years to use social media as a tool to reach out to LGBT*Q+ individuals (particularly teenagers and young adults) who were struggling with coming out or subjected to bullying.

> I was riding a train to JFK Airport when it occurred to me that I was waiting for permission that I no longer needed. In the era of social media—in a world with YouTube and Twitter and Facebook—I could speak directly to LGBT kids right now. I didn't need permission from parents or an invitation from a school. I could look into a camera, share my story, and let LGBT kids know that it got better for me and it would get better for them too. I could give 'em hope. (Savage and Miller 2012, 4)

In the last line of this quote, Savage is specifically conjuring memories of Harvey Milk by referencing their famous "Give 'em hope" speech from 1977 (Shilts 2008). Both of these men, even though separated by decades, were hoping to intervene with an ongoing and consistent issue for young people within the LGBT*Q+ community, which is a high rate of suicide and attempted suicide (Remafedi, Farrow, and Deisher 1991). In Milk's speech, he states that this hope can be accomplished by the election of openly gay politicians, which can serve as a signal to this at-risk population that, to reference *A Chorus Line*, they did not have to think that "being gay meant being a bum all the rest of [their lives]" (Attenborough 1985).

Milk hoped to serve as a role model to gradually change public perception, whereas Savage's approach desired something unique to our digital age to occur—a groundswell of digital affective action to help those in need in a rapid and instantaneous manner. Permission and time are no longer required or desired. The barriers for entry into producing content for social media are negligible, as almost 90 percent of individuals in the United States own a smartphone—more than the percentage who choose to engage with social media (Smith 2017). Not just limited to hearing messages about how life would get better, social media has been shown to offer many other affordances, such as allowing for individuals to create their own coming-out videos, dating, and even virtual support groups (Pullen and Cooper 2010). Despite the best of intentions, not everyone is afforded the same exposure and representation. In a study of the It Gets Better (IGB) campaign, Wight discovered many identities that were difficult to find, creating a new hegemony and further silencing an already minimized population, particularly those who are bisexual or trans* (2014).[3] This was not necessarily the fault of Savage, per se, but rather the network logics of YouTube in which more popular videos of famous individuals get more circulation than others (Wight 2014). In a society where the loudest get the most attention, those who are at the margins are oft overlooked, ignored, or silenced.

Behind the IGB's message is a reinforcement of the neoliberal logic that it is up to the oppressed individual to take on the responsibility of "picking themselves up by their bootstraps" and improving their own lives. The videos focus on individualistic message throughout: "tough it up until you are in a position in which you are able to come out" (Savage and Miller 2012). The full title of Savage's book is *It Gets Better: Coming Out, Overcoming Bullying, and Creating a Life Worth Living.* Embedded within the title lies the neoliberal notion that one is responsible for creating their own life worth living, essentially focusing the attention and onus onto individuals rather than on the collective. A "life worth living," often a vague expression, thus has a very specific definition: it is a life that conforms to the rest of society (minus gender or sexual identity) and contributes in a productive way to that society. In what is the epitome of what Duggan has referred to as "homonormativity," this message no longer remains one of radical change, but encourages assimilation.

> This New Homonormativity comes equipped with a rhetorical recoding of key terms in the history of gay politics: "equality" becomes narrow, formal access to a few conservatizing institutions, "freedom" becomes impunity for bigotry and vast inequalities in commercial life and civil society, the "right to privacy" becomes domestic confinement, and democratic politics itself becomes something to be escaped. All of this adds up to a corporate culture managed by a minimal state, achieved by the neoliberal privatization of affective as well as economic and public life. (Duggan 2002, 190)

Rather than radically changing the system for everyone, the agenda that Duggan critiques is one that aims to slightly adjust the system to allow LGBT*Q+ individuals to squeeze in. Even though both projects are about hope, they are about a very different kind of hope, a difference that Muñoz

(2009) describes as a hope for the future versus a hope for the present, and a hope based almost entirely on the affective labor of the LGBT*Q+ community and asking little of the rest of society.

Much work that has been done on the uses of social media of LGBT*Q+ individuals has largely been quantitative in nature to understand the ways it is being used (Pullen and Cooper 2010; Gudelunas 2012; Craig and McInroy 2014b), while not addressing the complex issues of society and culture. Other work, such as Jessica Lingel's (2017) necessary intervention in the use of social media for countercultures, focuses on niche members of the community, such as drag queens. In the early- to mid-2010s Facebook enacted a policy that required people to use their real or "authentic" identity and name on the site. This prompted many drag queens (as well as countless trans* and Native American individuals) to lose their profiles or be blocked (Grinberg 2014; Boyd 2012; Wilson 2015; Holpuch 2015). Lingel also discusses the fatigue that often plagues drag performers, both in relationship to the constant need for new material due to the pressure to post regularly and share video of routines as well as the amount of drama that resulted within the community (2017). In this way, social media, particularly Facebook, have fundamentally changed the way drag queens perform their craft and live as their alter-ego/stage personas.

Connection and intimacy have been a dominant focus of queer communication studies (Howard 2001; Bérubé 2003; McGlotten 2013; Muñoz 2009; Grov et al. 2014; Reddick 2012; O'Riordan and Phillips 2007; Race 2015; T. Dean 2008; Bonner-Thompson 2017). Much of these have focused on the sexual connection between two (or more) men, which is logical as much political discourse about the LGBT*Q+ rights movement focuses on male-to-male sexual activity (Frank 2013; Johnson and Holmes 2017; Redding 2008). Gay men have largely been at the forefront of incorporating new technology into locating their next sexual encounter (McGlotten 2013). While sexual intimacy is often at the center of a (particularly) gay, male identity, it is not the only or often even main component of ones' identity.

Sex is a part of the LGBT*Q+ community, and in some ways defines all identities within the community. Even for asexual individuals the lack of sexual desire is a key element of identity. As some of the individuals I spoke with testified, their own sexual desires from an early age shaped who they are and how they view themselves. This book breaks new ground by not focusing on merely understanding how individuals are using social media, but by examining social media use from a more holistic approach and deconstructing the idea of maintaining control over the disclosure of ones SOGI. It is also a reconceptualization of how we view the notion of coming out and identity, and what that means in an online world. Baym and boyd (2012) use the term "socially mediated publicness" to describe the ways that social media has ultimately changed the way we view the notion of public life and blurred the lines between public and private. In some regards, much of what is private has been made public—shared on our Instagram accounts, Facebook walls, and Snapchat stories. Yet, social media at the same time allows for private exploration of SOGI in ways never before allowed. It has allowed individuals to play with their sexual and gender expressions in the privacy of isolated and discrete corners of the online world. This has led to new research being done on the queerness of internet studies (Gieseking, Lingel, and Cockayne 2018). This project seeks to contribute to this ongoing and important conversation by not "treat[ing] the medium of delivery—television, radio, film, the internet, and so on—as neutral, universal, or presumptively masculine" (Shaw and Sender 2016, 1), nor by ascribing total influence to the medium. Rather than viewing social media as just a tool to be used, this book examines the positive and negative world-making possibilities that exist within these networks. It explores the affordances offered to individuals in understanding their identities, the influences society and media has on those, as well as the new and old risks posed by these online spaces.

THE RITUALIZATION OF SOCIAL MEDIA

Despite being heralded as a necessity for emotional well-being, the actual act of coming out is often discussed in scholarly and political settings in a somewhat sterile, pragmatic way. It is described as necessary to lead a fulfilling life and for societal change, as a way out of the hopelessness that is cast upon those who are not out. However, the act itself is full of emotions: anxiety, fear, hope, happiness, and sadness. In the traditional way of coming out (i.e., in person to one's family or friends), all parties involved experience these emotions simultaneously. Expanding this experience into the digital and social media, we must consider new questions of affect. As Ahmed points out, texts have emotions, which can lead to other emotions in other bodies (Ahmed, 2015). Not only do texts have emotions, but certain objects—and, by extension, images—have specific connotations or affects that stick to them more than others (Ahmed, 2015; Puar, 2007). While these connotations and emotions can change based on historical situations, the LGBT*Q+ community is one that has had numerous connotations stuck to it. As Kitzinger reminds us, during the late 1980s throughout the 1990s the LGBT*Q+ community as a whole became synonymous with sickness and death because of the AIDS epidemic (Kitzinger, 1999). This specific connotation may not be quite as prevalent, but the connotations attached to groups or objects are essentially emotions that become linked to those affecting the way individuals can interact with them.

Coming out has become almost synonymous with a positive and happy emotion that it essentially unlocks in oneself. Rather than remaining just a political necessity, coming out has become framed as a pathway toward personal happiness and self-fulfillment (Savage & Miller, 2012). Specifically, an individual and personal happiness in the present moment or near future. This focus on personal happiness and fulfillment focuses on optimism about the present, rather than pessimism about the current state of affairs, which Ahmed (2015) states is important for political revolution. It is only by envisioning and fighting for a utopic future that true liberation can occur (Muñoz, 2009). This focus on happiness is also related to a turn toward respectability politics among the LGBT*Q+ movement with its focus on marriage and other heteronormative values. These discourses have stripped from the movement much of its radical potential drawn from its negative emotions of the past (Cvetkovich, 2012; Duggan, 2002; Muñoz, 2009).

Social media is, at its core, a series of discourses filtered through the logics of the various platforms and the audiences who interact with them. Accepting Foucault's (1969) claim that discourse forms reality, the discursive practices that happen online impact the worlds of those who create them. These discourses are not unfiltered or naturally occurring, but rather are subject to logics that are inherent to the platforms (Castells 2010; Sampson 2012). It is because of this latter reason that, even though trans* stories exist within IGB, they are not easily found because of the sorting and recommendation features of YouTube (Wight 2014). In this way, we must consider all decisions that factor into a social media platform and treat them as political actions, which can affect the way that discourses place out, and therefore alter the reality of some individuals.

Foucault points out that discourse needs to be understood as more than just language or signs, but needs to include "practices that systematically form the objects of which they speak" (1969, 49). These practices are not limited to content posted online but include the ways people interact with these platforms, including making decisions on what to share and not to share. In this way, expressions of sexual and gender identity (SOGI) are discursive practices that are not only the actual expressions but also the societal framing of them. One must turn to religion, especially the Protestant undertones that have shaped and formed US societal norms and culture to understand the demands and constraints placed upon expressions of SOGI.

Foucault related discussion of sexuality with the confession in that it is the one who lives outside of the societal norms who is forced to confess their "sins" (Foucault 1990). As Ahmed (2006) points out, within US culture there is a norm of compulsory heterosexuality that prescribes a path leading toward marriage and family rearing. Unless confessed otherwise, it is assumed one is heterosexual and it is only when the heterosexual is in the minority that they deem it necessary to come out. Despite the liberatory power proscribed to individuals by coming out (and on the individual basis this may be correct), by aligning with and using the normative terms of the discourse, the actual act might help to reinforce the hegemony of heterosexuality. Since it is only that which is deviant that must be confessed, the act of public coming out confirms its place in the minds of many of the abnormality of non-cis-heterosexual identities. As C. Wright Mills stated:

> Any establishment of culture means the establishment of definitions of reality, values, taste. . . . Debate is limited. Only certain views are allowed. But more than that, the terms of debate, the terms in which the world may be seen, the standards, and lack of standards by which men judge their accomplishments of themselves, and of other men—these terms are officially or commercially determined, inculcated, enforced. (1972, 412–13)

Hall (1980) posits that audiences have a multitude of ways to decode or interpret messages received including one that is oppositional to the dominant/hegemonic reading. One of the key points in Hall's theory is that all messages are decoded in the terms of the dominant message, which, if we take Mills's statement about needing to change the terms of debate seriously, could limit the effectiveness of resistance (Hall 1980; Mills 1972).

It is important, when considering resistance in the LGBT*Q+ community to examine various performative acts in which individuals are engaged in resisting. Muñoz, in his work on disidentification, references Gramsci's notion of a war of position, and how "the more multilayered and tactical war of positions represents better possibilities of resistance today, when discriminatory ideologies are less naked and more intricate" (1999, 114). Specifically talking about performers who subtly call into question societal norms, Muñoz describes a way of opposition that serves to challenge and undermine mainstream assumptions about groups of individuals to bring about subtle change. Challenging cultural norms and assumptions of the LGBT*Q+ community was an important element for most of the individuals I spoke with throughout my interviews for this project in deciding what to share online. These desires to challenge cis-heteronormative values and to provide help for others within the LGBT*Q+ community largely influenced the way that they engaged with social media.

Couldry states that we should view media as ritual and practice, rather than as objects separate from the ways in which individuals interact with them. The content, the platforms, and the individuals who use them all inform each other and shape both the way they function and the way they influence the lives of individuals.

> By moving media research's centre of gravity away from texts (and their production or direct reception) and towards the broader set of *practices* related to media, we get a better grip on the distinctive types of *social processes* enacted *through* media related practices, practices involving not just producer and performers but also interactive audiences, audience members who would

like to become performers, and non-viewing members of the public who become affected by that wider process. (Couldry 2012, 44)

This is useful for two main reasons. The first is that it extends the audience
beyond those directly affected by the viewing or creation of media artifact to
those who are affected in general by the way media enter the larger public
discourse. The second is that by viewing media as ritual we are able to draw
into question the role and influence of power, because "rituals are enactments
of power through form" (Couldry 2012, 66). As Foucault reminds us, power
is not unidirectional, only coming from the top down, but that it always
includes resistance that lies within power (1990). This is important to remember in relationship to social media, because it helps to counteract the
"myth of the mediated center," or the notion that media is central to culture,
since if media is a ritual performed by the interactions between audience and
medium there is no set center (Couldry 2012; Hoover 2006). As Shaw elucidated in her study of video games, it was often only through a negotiation of
identities between the game characters and the players that meaning was able
to be negotiated for the audience (Shaw 2015).

Viewing media as ritual highlights the patterned and repetitive nature of
the way many interact. When considering social media and what posts are
shared, it is important to consider how naturalized or ritualized this process
has become and what this means. To state that media usage is ritualized is not
to assume that is has become invisible, as some might contend (Deuze 2011),
but rather to suggest that these practices have become an integral part into the
lives of many individuals.

UNDERSTANDING A SOCIAL MEDIA AGE

In an effort to understand the way that LGBT*Q+ individuals are integrating
social media into their daily lives, there were several questions that I wanted
to answer:

- What is the role of social media in *creating and/or reinforcing* a dominant
  LGBT*Q+ identity?
- Who is *included* in the dominant LGBT*Q+ community, and what effects
  does being *excluded* have on those individuals?
- What new *affordances* are offered by social media for individuals to ex-
  plore their sexual and/or gender identities?
- What potential *benefits or harm* can social media create in the lived expe-
  riences of LGBT*Q+ individuals?

And finally,

- What *forms of resistance and political expression* are made possible through social media discourse?

In order to begin to find some answers to these questions, it was important to me to attempt to gain a 360-degree vantage of how individuals are using social media in their daily lives. Building on both Couldry's (Dolan 2012) and Shaw's (2015) methodological approaches to understanding the ritual use of media, I employed multiple qualitative methods to examine these questions via a variety of angles and perspectives. As Shaw explained in her study of representation in video games:

> Games do not exist in a ludological vacuum, but neither can we ignore the extent to which play affects audience readings. We cannot look at representation by looking just at game texts, because the intertwined aspects of representation and play necessarily involve audiences' use of texts. Audiences matter, and as I argue, they are how representation comes to matter. (2015, 37)

To gain a 360-degree understanding of the influence of social media, I combined critical discourse analysis, visual communication analysis, and audience research that combined interviews and participant observation.

Due to the qualitative and multifaceted approach that I used to examine this topic, it was important to use grounded theory and a cyclical approach to coding the themes, categories, and concepts that emerged from the data (Saldaña 2013). Despite that I explain each method separately in this chapter, all research was conducted simultaneously. Therefore, the themes that emerged throughout the interviews or focus groups informed the categories I would later examine in the archival research and vice versa. These categories were then used to further examine the data, which were then further dissected and explored for more nuanced expressions (Corbin and Strauss 1990; Hallberg 2006; Saldaña 2013). It is through this iterative process that several key ideas, or salient categories, rose to prominence: the importance of (and a queer definition of) the political, the weight given to coming out, and the exclusionary discourses and practices exhibited by those within the LGBT*Q+ community.

Audience Research

Finding out how individuals were interacting with social media in their daily lives was important to understand the meaning behind the online creation of messages and how the audience interprets them. To do this, I interviewed twenty participants in a combination of group and individual interviews. Participants were selected through convenience sampling, recruitment in online LGBT*Q+ forums in the Denver metropolitan area, and snowball sampling methods. Denver was an interesting location to me due to its diversity in regard to geography of origin, political affiliation, and economic class. In the 2010s Denver became one of the fastest-growing large cities in the United States with individuals moving there from all over the world (Sevits 2018). Colorado has long been considered a purple state with many people not solely identifying entirely as Democrat or Republican, which leads to a wide variety of political opinions and ideologies. The state of Colorado is also relatively diverse in terms of ethnicity, with more than 20 percent of individuals identifying as either Latino or Hispanic (Karlik 2019). Additionally, several interviews were conducted via Skype with individuals from across the United States in order to help further diversify the participants. People were chosen based on their gender and sexual identities as well as other factors, such as age and ethnicity, to create a diverse participant group based on SOGI as well as other factors such as age and ethnicity to create a diverse participant group (see figure 1.1 and table 1.1). Due to some of the sensitive topics that came up in our discussions, all individuals I interviewed did so under the condition of anonymity, and pseudonyms will be used for each of the interviewees in this book.

As Hoover and Clark pointed out, "it is clear that what people say reflects a set of received 'public scripts' which value certain kinds of media over others" (2008, 5). It is through this tension between what is said and what is practiced that societal norms and power make their presence known. When examining issues of representation on social media, it is crucial to understand

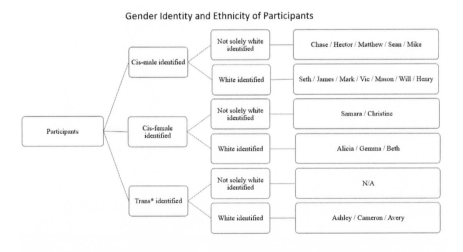

Gender Identity and Ethnicity of Participants

Figure 1.1.   Gender and Ethnicity of Participants. All individuals are anonymous and pseudonyms are used. Created by Patrick M. Johnson. 2019.

Table 1.1. Sexual Orientation of Participants. All individuals are anonymous and pseudonyms are used. Created by Patrick M. Johnson. 2019.

Gay	Lesbian	Bisexual	Asexual	Polysexual	Queer
Seth	Beth	Alicia	Gemma	Avery	Cameron
James	Ashley	Henry			
Chase	Christine				
Hector	Samara				
Matthew					
Mark					
Sean					
Vic					
Mason					
Will					
Mike					

how people are actually using the platforms, rather than a presentation of idealized usage. Each interview followed an informal conversation in which the participants demonstrated and described their social media usage. These conversations walked through each platform that the participants used and what they used them for. During this time the participants would show examples of each platform, including the content they produced as well as what they consumed. After the observation, each participant then participated in a semi-structured interview that focused on how they used social media around their various coming-out experiences and how it may have changed when switching between the various phases.

Visual Discourse Analysis

To supplement the voices of my participants, I analyzed numerous LGBT*Q+-specific media, both historical and contemporary, to examine the way certain narratives become highlighted. I examined 330 historical articles, images, and advertisements from LGBT*Q+ periodicals from the 1940s to the early 2000s stored in the New York Public Library's Lesbian, Gay, Bisexual, and Transgender collection and in the Smithsonian Museum of American History's Archives Center Lesbian, Gay, Bisexual, Transgender Collection, 1915–2016. In addition to the historical archives, each participant provided me with access to their social media profiles on the various sites and apps that they used. I recruited many participants from various LGBT*Q+ Facebook groups, including "LGBT*Q+ Professionals," "Queer Denver Exchange," and "Thick Latinos and their Admirers."

In addition to analyzing content in the three aforementioned groups, I analyzed twelve candid coming-out videos on YouTube, constituting over three hours of coming-out footage. These were discovered initially using the search term "Coming Out Live" and then allowing the YouTube algorithms to auto-play the next video. The muddied ethics of social media have been debated by scholars and journalists alike, and there is no clear consensus as how we as scholars of media should approach these topics. I have chosen to include my analyses of these venues for two main reasons. The first is that I have taken every effort to assure the privacy of individuals in situations where the group is a closed group that I belonged to before beginning on this research journey. Rather than analyzing and dissecting individual posts, I have looked only to get the larger picture of what was going on in the discourse in order to frame and corroborate the information provided by my interview participants. The second is that these moments and sites of discourse feature prominently in framing the experiences and worldviews of individuals within the LGBT*Q+ community. They were not created with the intent to be analyzed, but as pointed out in studies of IGB, they often have real-world consequences—particularly for the most marginalized members of the LGBT*Q+ community. It is thus crucial that social media content that is shared in some matter of a public way, whether that be a closed group or open to the public, be examined to see the cultural and political work that is being done within it.

Using open coding, I analyzed these images and texts to determine the themes that were consistent within them to determine the ways they help to shape reality (Corbin and Strauss 1990; Hallberg 2006; Rose 2012; Urquhart, Lehmann, and Myers 2009). Visuals have the ability of:

> producing specific visions of social difference—of hierarchies of class, race, gender, sexuality, and so on—while itself claiming not to be part of that hierarchy and thus to be universal. It is because this ordering of difference depends on a distinction between those who claim to see with universal and those who are seen to be categorized in particular ways, that Haraway claims it is intimately related to the oppressions and tyrannies of capitalism, colonialism, patriarchy, and so on. (Rose 2012, 9)

Christmann (2008) explains the need to examine photographs and visuals on multiple levels because rather than capturing reality they are always subjected to cultural influences. No image is separate from reality, despite the perceived objectivity of some. As Sontag points out, a photograph implies a sense of reality as it contains a trace of the real and is far more than just an interpretation (Sontag 2001). Some believe the relationship of photographic images with reality is starting to replace the real world with an image world or a media life (Deuze 2011; Sontag 2001). Visuals function as a performative language that they re-create, reinforce, or even craft their own reality in the same way that acts of language can act to codify and organize the world (Culler 2011). Images thus simultaneously reflect, create, and shed light on the cultural mores and norms in which they were produced (Christmann 2008; Hasenmueller 1978; Knoblauch et al. 2008; Panofsky 1972).

In this view, when examining visuals, the concern is not the exact content or authorial intent of each visual, but rather the social production of the images and their impact on the lived experiences of individuals. Discourse analysis is also not concerned with looking for one solid narrative, but is open to exploring discourses that are both complex and contradictory (Rose 2012). Through this project I am not making any claims to universal truth, but rather attempting to point to an interpretation of these narratives, while aware that my interpretations are also part of this narrative.

Bird noted that, "methods matter because the choices made along, with the very characteristics of the researcher, play into and ultimately shape the conclusions of any research" (2003, 9). As Shaw stated, "methods are central, not peripheral to our arguments" (2015, 42). Rather than merely being a means to an end, the research methods used are essential to the conclusions that I reached and the arguments that I propose throughout this text.

As is the case with many marginalized groups, those in the LGBT*Q+ community are often unable to represent themselves or make their voices heard. As DeVault and Gross explain,

> the traditions of research interviewing have been strongly linked to social justice concerns and projects and to the idea of bringing forward neglected voices—and these traditions continue to be especially important for feminist projects. (2012, 9)

It is with this notion of highlighting and bringing to light the voices of LGBT*Q+ individuals who do not always have this opportunity that the voices of my participants prominently feature in this book. In addition to understanding the role that social media has in expressions of LGBT*Q+ culture, politics, and identity, a secondary goal of this project is to capture and share the stories and experiences of a cross-section of the LGBT*Q+ community.

LGBT*Q+ individuals often feel a sense of social isolation, which can lead to greater instances of mental health issues and suicide (Remafedi, Farrow, and Deisher 1991; J. K. Puar 2012; Carosone 2013; Asala 2010; The Trevor Project 2019). With the development of social media over the past several decades, two things have become clear. The world is more connected than it has ever been, which allows LGBT*Q+ individuals living in areas where they might otherwise feel isolated connect with others like them. This can help to ease that sense of loneliness and despair that have plagued the community for decades. At the same time that connections have grown closer, social media has also led to increases in the same types of bullying and exclusion that have pervaded the LGBT*Q+ community, both from outside and within the community. Often considered safe and welcoming spaces to find your identity, they are often also spaces of marginalization and tokenization. Rather than only looking at one side of this issue, in this book I explore and shine a light on the ways that social media is at times both a beacon of hope for some and a site of exclusion for others.

OVERVIEW

Before beginning to comprehend the role that social media is having within the LGBT*Q+ community, it is important to understand the way that LGBT*Q+ media has worked to shape contemporary culture. Chapter 2 provides an analysis of the historical trajectory of LGBT*Q+ periodicals in shaping current norms within the LGBT*Q+ community, particularly in the emphasis on coming-out narratives and the belief that LGBT*Q+ individuals must be politically informed and active. I also examine the ways that images, classifieds, and editorials worked to shape and reinforce ideas of attractiveness and desirability within the gay community. Moreover, I explore the historical emphasis on gay men at the exclusion of bisexual, lesbian, trans*, and asexual individuals.

Chapter 3 interrogates how social media is factoring into the coming-out process for LGBT*Q+ individuals. I start by raising questions about assumptions of what it means to come out and the ways that we should consider it a continual process rather than a discrete event. Through analyzing a series of candid coming-out videos and posts about coming out, I examine the way these new technologies work to reinforce a "proper" ritual of coming out. These often only focus on certain narratives and ignore many factors that can complicate this process. Finally, this chapter works to shed light on some of the new risks and anxieties caused by sharing content on social media, especially for LGBT*Q+ teens and young adults and those already marginalized within the community.

Politics have long been an important aspect of the LGBT*Q+ community, and chapter 4 explores the ways that social media is changing political discourse. By focusing on the technological affordances that enable political discourse to spread to more individuals, I demonstrate how the precarious positionality of LGBT*Q+ individuals can expand typical notions of what it means to be politically active. For a community that is often invisible and at heightened risk for suicide, health disparities, and violence, the LGBT*Q+ community have shown a heightened emphasis on a politics of visibility and survival.

Chapter 5 focuses on the exclusionary tactics toward marginalized members within the LGBT*Q+ community, particularly trans* and HIV-positive individuals as well as LGBT*Q+ individuals of color. These include both active acts of aggression as well as microaggressions that many individuals report dealing with on a regular basis. In addition to examining the exclusion of certain individuals, I also explore the policing of what individuals share under the guise of demanding authenticity.

The conclusion focuses on the ways that social media both provides new affordances to help individuals in expressing their gender and sexual identities to themselves and to others, as well as creates new anxieties and fears around these expressions. I also provide guidelines for individuals within the LGBT*Q+ community to consider when using social media. Lastly, I include a list of things that social media developers should consider regarding how their decisions affect the way LGBT*Q+ individuals interact with each other.

Finally, in the afterword, I reflect on my role in the process of creating this collection of stories and insights. I also consider some new developments that have occurred within the world of social media, focusing largely on the gay app Grindr's Kindr initiative that was created in an attempt to combat some of the negative interactions on that app. Finally, I reflect on the role that social media should have in forging a new queer politics, informed by the individuals who so kindly shared their stories with me.

NOTES

1. The acronym to represent the LGBT*Q2SIAA community has changed constantly and consistently throughout the decades that have followed in the wake of the Stonewall Riots. For consistency and simplicity purposes, throughout this book LGBT*Q+ will be used to represent any iteration of the acronym. Many of the additions to this acronym are often the result of an attempt to raise political visibility of one group that has been historically excluded from the mainstream movement. For example, 2S stands for "two-spirit" and is intended to raise awareness and inclusion for the indigenous populations who have been marginalized in the United States since the arrival of the colonists. Since, in my definition, "queer" refers not to a sexuality or gender identity, but instead is a political and personal ideology that, at its core, is about marginalization and resisting hetero-cis-patriarchal norms of society it can encompass all the other addendums to the acronym for this diverse and widespread community.

2. Since the 2008 US presidential election, the use of the term mainstream media became commonplace and now has a plethora of definitions in the way that it is used. For the purposes of this book, the term mainstream refers to anything that is not explicitly and primarily for LGBT*Q+ individuals. Many of these "mainstream" sites are frequently used and enjoyed by LGBT*Q+ individuals, and they often offer content for them (e.g., *Will & Grace* on NBC), but the space is not primarily for them. For this reason, LGBT*Q+ spaces will be referred to as LGBT*Q+ or queer spaces and all others will be referred to as mainstream spaces.

3. Trans* is used to refer to the umbrella category that includes those individuals who are not cisgender. This includes those who identity as transgender, transsexual, nonbinary, agender, etc.

Chapter Two

Creation of a Hegemonic LGBT*Q+ Culture

In the late portion of the twentieth century and into the early twenty-first century, representations of LGBT*Q+ characters in mainstream media surged to levels that had never before been seen (R. Becker 2006; GLAAD 2017; Russo 1987). In addition to the inclusion of LGBT*Q+ characters in popular television shows, films, news, and even comic books, there has also been an increase in shows produced for and by the LGBT*Q+ community. Moreover, these shows do not just merely exist, they have started winning major industry accolades. Examples include shows such as *RuPaul's Drag Race* winning multiple Emmy awards including one for best Reality Competition Show and films such as *Moonlight* winning numerous prestigious awards including an Academy Award for Best Motion Picture. Despite the recent increased visibility of LGBT*Q+-geared media existing in the mainstream, this community has produced a significant amount of content for decades (even pre-dating the official rise of the LGBT*Q+ rights movement in 1969) in magazines, pamphlets, and other periodicals.

A HISTORY OF SECRECY

Examining the history of LGBT*Q+ publications within the United States necessarily requires considering the laws and policies that regulated the openness with which one could live as an LGBT*Q+ individual. While gay and lesbian men and women have formed communities within the United States since the late 1800s (Chauncey 1994), it has only been in recent (since the early 2000s) history that anti-sodomy laws have largely been struck down, effectively eliminating the criminalization of homosexuality. In fact, for much of LGBT*Q+ history in the United States, one could be arrested, harassed, or even fired on the mere suspicion or accusation of being homosexual. For this reason, much communication that existed within the LGBT*Q+ community was done under a guise of secrecy—meeting in secret bars, bathhouses, public parks, and through various media (Bérubé 2003; Chauncey 1994; D'Emilio 1998; Meeker 2006). As a result, many of the early publications preceding the LGBT*Q+ rights movement of the 1970s were covertly targeted toward gay men. Lesbian women during the decades around the two world wars were still largely confined by societal restrictions, which all but required them to enter into heterosexual marriages and prohibited them from being financially independent enough to go to bars or other spaces of their own. This led to much of lesbian culture at the time being centered around small events in their homes with just a lover and/or a small group of friends, which "structured a view that one's sexuality [was] an exclusively private matter" (D'Emilio 1998, 33).

Prior to the landmark *One, Inc. v. Olesen* case in 1958, any periodical that was overtly geared toward the gay and lesbian community was considered obscene (Ball 2015). As such, many of these early publications were produced in secret and disguised as other forms of magazines, such as the popular beefcake magazines published from the 1930s through the 1960s, which highlighted photographs of muscular men engaging in homoerotic sporting events (Rosenberg 2015). There were also "pornographic" magazines that were discreetly geared toward gay men (often posing as fitness magazines), personal magazines that allowed individuals to post advertisements for anonymous sexual encounters, and gay travel guides to point men toward gay bars, bathhouses, and cruising locations.

In light of these communication outlets, gay men, contrary to lesbian women, developed a more public community around meeting in secretive bars and cruising for anonymous sex in parks, bathrooms, and truck stops (Chauncey 1994; D'Emilio 1998; Howard 2001). It was through these initial forms of gathering that some of the first homophile organizations began to form in the 1950s. These organizations began publishing their own flyers and newsletters to keep individuals informed about issues affecting gays and lesbians as well as to promote political involvement (D'Emilio 1998; Stewart-Winter 2016). There were thus two main forms of gay and lesbian publications produced within the 1950s and early 1960s:

1. those focused on promoting political action and community engagement (e.g., *The Mattachine Review*), and
2. those focused on sexual pleasure and entertainment (e.g., *Blue Notes-Flash: The National Magazine of Gay Correspondence*).

These two worlds would eventually merge in the late 1960s in the aftermath of the Lavender Scare[1] in the McCarthy era as the intensity of police raids of gay bars increased (Johnson 2004; Shilts 2008). In 1967 *The Advocate* (which is still a popular LGBT*Q+ magazine) formed in response to the harassment occurring in gay spaces. This intended to create a widespread gay and lesbian publication that focused on political and social issues pertinent to the community.

In addition to providing relevant information for the LGBT*Q+ community, an important element of *The Advocate* in its early days was to provide a space to foster the growth of personal connections and relationships. In every issue of the publication there was a secondary classifieds section, which was equal in size and length to the more journalistic front section. These classified sections and personal ads, along with the travel guides published at the time, provided opportunities for communities of gay and lesbian individuals to form, an important element in creating a more cohesive idea of a community around something as ethereal as sexuality. As Martin Meeker elucidated in his study of gay and lesbian communications within the early to mid-1900s:

> The projects of articulating identities and building communities, however, are not ones that many homosexuals chose with purpose or foresight. Indeed, the entire process was fraught because for boys, girls, men, and women who desired contacts there was neither innate knowledge nor a handbook given to them that shared the steps that must [be] taken to achieve an identity and find a community. Yet, a connection had to be made, and throughout the twentieth century an apparently increasing number of individuals possessed a burning desire to connect. (2006, 1–2)

LGBT*Q+ communities, since their inceptions, have always placed much importance on personal connections. This emphasis worked to shape and form many aspects now considered to be staples of contemporary LGBT*Q+ culture.

One of the ways these connections historically formed was through gay and lesbian publications. These publications thus became important not only to provide an outlet for communication, but since they also served to educate and entertain the public, it is my contention that they became influential in working to shape the way the culture formed. Through their decisions on which topics were covered, the political leanings they indicated, and images used by these periodicals, they began to frame the issues and ideas that became foundational among the newly blossoming LGBT*Q+ community (Scheufele 1999). Most mainstream portrayals of the gay and lesbian community at this time were largely negative or treated as a wholly foreign culture within journalistic outlets (D'Emilio 1998; Howard 2001; Meeker 2006; Russo 1987). Rising up to critique mainstream representations,

LGBT*Q+-specific outlets formed to highlight "positive" portrayals, promote political activity relevant to the LGBT*Q+ community, and support entertainment venues such as bars and nightclubs.

Even as mainstream representations of the LGBT*Q+ community increased (particularly in the 1990s and 2000s), the need for LGBT*Q+-specific publications and media maintained a strong importance within the community (R. Becker 2006; Eaklor 2008; Henderson 2013). One of the issues with much of the mainstream representation of LGBT*Q+ individuals is that it often relied (and arguably continues to rely) on stereotypical and unidimensional representations of what it means to be gay, lesbian, transgender, etc. As Lisa Henderson points out in her text "Love and Money," even when these are seemingly positive representations (as became more commonplace throughout the early 2000s) they still often work to celebrate only a certain type of queerness while chastising and ridiculing others (2013).

> Queer class distinction is visible through four gestures across a range of forms and genres: (1) good queers (protagonists, familiars) are moved from the class margins to the class middle, where practices of bodily control are maximized; (2) bad queerness and powerlessness are represented as class marginality and are signified by performative excess and failures of physical control; (3) wealth becomes the expression of fabulousness, in a limited version of the good life legitimately achieved; and (4) class is displaced onto family and familialism as the locus of normalcy and civic viability. (Henderson 2013, 34)

While this critique is largely levied toward mainstream representations (e.g., *Modern Family*, *Will & Grace*, *The L Word*, *Queer as Folk*) that target a predominantly heterosexual or mixed audience, it is my contention that these class distinctions are prevalent within the LGBT*Q+ community and many have their origins within gay and lesbian publications created by and for the LGBT*Q+ community. While the scope of this chapter will focus largely on LGBT*Q+-specific publications, it is important to also consider the representations that occur within mainstream media and especially those that span many types of media.

The importance of this became relevant to me as many of these publications, and LGBT*Q+-specific media in general, came up in the interviews and observations that I conducted. Even though the interviews centered on "social media" and many of the participants came out in the age of social media, the importance of legacy or traditional media was often referenced as heavily influencing their perceptions of LGBT*Q+ culture and identity. This ranged from reading articles about films and movies containing fourth-persona textual winks to LGBT*Q+ individuals (Ott and Mack 2014) to using personal ads to find dates and/or anonymous sexual encounters. As was indicated in almost every interview, as well as in my own personal coming-out experience, media representations not only provide a lens to view the perceptions of others (as a whole) of the LGBT*Q+ community and help shape one's own personality; they are additionally useful tools to gauge others' specific reactions when planning to disclose one's SOGI.

To better understand the importance of social media on public declarations of SOGI and LGBT*Q+ culture and politics, it is necessary then to analyze and examine the historical trajectory that has influenced contemporary LGBT*Q+ culture. I examined numerous periodicals, comics, and other publications produced by and for the LGBT*Q+ community ranging from the late 1950s to the early 2000s in two different historical archives: the "Lesbian, Gay, Bisexual and Transgender Periodical Collection 1952–1999" at the New York Public Library and the Archives Center Lesbian, Gay, Bisexual, Transgender Collection, 1915–2016 at the Smithsonian Institution. Forty-five boxes, each containing between forty to eighty issues of periodicals[2] were examined, specifically, to trace and analyze the way the discourses within the LGBT*Q+ community formed and changed over time. Using grounded theory, extensive notes were kept on the main themes discovered within each periodical (Corbin and Strauss 1990; Hallberg 2006; Urquhart, Lehmann, and Myers 2009). From these periodicals, 352 articles/media artifacts were randomly selected, ensuring that the sources represented the vast diversity in types of publications and target audiences (see table 2.1). Applying discursive analysis methods, open coding, and building on the themes discovered within the periodicals, each article was analyzed and coded (Corbin and Strauss 1990; Flick, Kardorff, and Steinke 2010; Gill 2000; Lindlof 2011).

Several prominent themes emerged throughout the analysis: importance of personal connections, an emphasis on political activism, representations of stereotypes, and discussion of divisions within the LGBT*Q+ community. Each will be examined in more depth throughout this chapter.

IMPORTANCE OF CONNECTIONS

A common sentiment within the LGBT*Q+ community has been that since there is no guarantee of familial acceptance or love, especially historically, it is crucial to form our own families and communities. This emphasis on finding and forging loving and supporting connections is especially evident when examining the place of importance that personal ads occupied within the early days of gay and lesbian periodicals. While there had long been an emphasis on connections, through coded language, bars, private gatherings, book clubs, and public sex (Chauncey 1994; D'Emilio 1998; Howard 2001; Meeker 2006), new avenues for connections fueled by technological and media innovations changed the ways that the LGBT*Q+ community could connect (Meeker 2006).

Table 2.1. LGBT*Q+ Periodicals in the United States. List of LGBT*Q+ periodicals analyzed from the LGBT+ Archives at the National Museum of American History and the New York Public Library, 1945–2015. Created by Patrick M. Johnson. 2019.

LGBT*Q+ Periodicals, 1945–2015

AIDS Awareness Cards	Bay Area Gay Liberation	Bay Times
BL	Black & White Men Together Quarterly	Black Lace
Blacklight	Blood Brothers	Blue Notes
Bondings	Boonies: A Voice for Rural Gays	Boston Gayline
California Scene	Clique Magazine	Come Out
Compete	Eye to Eye: Portraits of Lesbians	Gay Comix
Gay Liberation Supplement	Gay Life	Gay Parent
Go	Holy Titclamps	Ikons
Making a Way: Lesbians Out Front	Man's Way	Queerly Divine
RFD	S.T.H.	Swerv
Swerve	The Advocate	The Barb
The Bi-Sexual Expression	Liberation News	

SWM Seeks Similar for Fun and Friendship

Due to the importance of forming connections within the community, many popular magazines included large classified/personal sections (half of the content for *The Advocate* at this time was classifieds) and even entire magazines dedicated to nothing except for forming these connections. *Blue Notes-Flash* (*Blue Notes-Flash* n.d.), for example, labeled themselves "the national magazine of gay correspondence" and also guaranteed a circulation of "over 135,000" people. The magazine, which consists entirely of two- to four-sentence classified ads and only one picture on the cover, also assured to its audience that both the readers and contributors would provide "total secrecy and confidentiality." Published in and distributed from Miami, Florida, *Blue Notes* was mailed out as a companion magazine to *Blueboy* magazine but was additionally available for individual purchase within adult bookstores across the nation. Most of the ads were purely sexual in nature and the magazine was entirely male-centric, featuring ads such as:

CA-1072–92064
San Diego CA area. Wants to meet Marines,

Sailors, truck drivers, hair chested men,
etc. I am W/M 39, 6,' 170lbs. Nude photo a
must. (*Blue Notes-Flash* n.d.)

And

AL-1003–35216–0
White male, 135 lbs., young, well built,
handsome. Want sex from slim, well built,
hairy guys, 18–28 in Birmingham area. Race
unimportant. No hustlers, fems. Send recent
photo. Will answer all letters. (*Blue Notes-Flash* n.d., 1)

Confidentiality and discretion are key themes within the majority of the ads found in this periodical and others like it—indicating the new possibilities of intimate connections created by these magazines. Whereas discreet sexual encounters had been a long-standing component of the gay community, it was not without danger (Chauncey 1994; Howard 2001; Shilts 2008). Cruising for sex in public parks, bathrooms, and even gay bathhouses and bars did provide opportunities for connections between men, but this activity, regardless of location, was always accompanied by a danger of being arrested, assaulted (by the police and/or others), or publicly outed (Shilts 2008). The ability to discreetly meet men through a third-party "middleman" likely provided a sense of safety and security to many individuals to explore their sexuality in ways they could not do so previously. Rather than a risky public encounter, gay men could now meet men in safer more private locations—important considerations for individuals whose jobs would have depended on remaining in the closet, such as politicians, military members, or even teachers.

Beyond just providing a new venue for sexual encounters, these magazines also became a place to meet friends and potential long-term lovers. More than just providing alternative outlets for anonymous sexual encounters, these magazines were providing alternatives to anonymous sexual encounters:

CA-25424–90048
L.A. area: 31-year-old white Sagittarian tired
of bar scenes and one nite [*sic*] stands is hoping
to meet a guy (25–40) equally Fed-up. If we
have this much in common we might find a
relationship. Consider myself trim and good
looking. Please write and send photo if available. (*Blue Notes-Flash* n.d.)

While not as common as sexual ads, there was a noticeable emphasis on developing lasting relationships, which in addition to searching for companionship often included derogatory references toward the "cruising scene."

Beyond the classifieds, a major source of revenue for these periodicals was from groups and companies buying advertisements where they offered to provide individuals with matchmaking services. These ads often explained the importance and superiority of personal (i.e., face-to-face) connections over mediated ones. For example, one ad for GSF (a social networking company) from a 1977 edition of *The Advocate* advised people to "Get out of the 'meat' market, and meet people" (GSF 1977, 3). Offering to connect members who lived within Southern California and New York City with other "compatible sincere gay men and women . . . with whom you can build a truly meaningful relationship" (GSF 1977, 3), this advertisement appears on the surface to break many of the notions that flooded the typical classifieds sections for two main reasons. The first is that it was clearly speaking against casual hookups and the (perceived) lack of personal, deep, fulfilling connections resulting from bars and clubs. The second is that it seemed to be providing an outlet for both men and women to make connections, whereas other many of the periodicals (e.g., *Blue Notes*) catered solely to gay men, limiting the access of lesbian women to a nationwide network of peers as was readily available to gay men. Despite there being some options for lesbian women to form connections, they were not as open or frequent as the ones for gay men (Meeker 2006). While the ability to form relationships through mediated means did exist for the lesbian community, its limited nature often

> translated into a feeling of isolation and, consequently, the sense that they should seek out and connect with other lesbians, whether by moving to cities, participating in an organization, meeting a friend, exchanging letters, or simply reading a book or magazine. (Meeker 2006, 114)

Despite boasting in that advertisement that the service was for both men and women, it is clear by their revised ad a year later in 1978 who their true target demographic was. While the text remained unchanged (apart from expanding their service areas), the visual elements of the advertisement changed dramatically. Instead of simple black text on a white backdrop, the ad showcased white print against a black background with the word "MEN" in giant letters at the top. The bottom of the ad also included a black-and-white photograph of two shirtless, muscular men embracing in the entrance of a cave. Whereas the textual elements of this advertisement speak to an inclusive, relationship-focused dating service, the visual elements clearly indicate that this service is first and foremost a service for men to meet other men— most likely for sexual encounters.

The next year, the GSF advertisement changed its message once again, this time featuring a sketch of three, white men laughing with the heading "Making Friends." Albeit clearly geared toward forming friendships and long-lasting relationships, this advertisement notably removes all but one mention of women from the text: you can "choose from among thousands of exciting men & women" (GSF 1979). The advertisement becomes almost the exclusive property of gay men, where they are the priority and center of attention and women are there for mere decoration.

Despite being a popular magazine within the LGBT*Q+ community, *The Advocate* also directly promoted the superiority of personal connections and experiences over mediated ones. In 1978, *The Advocate* began advertising for and held an event they named *The Advocate* Experience. Despite *The Advocate*'s goal for individuals to read and be informed, this event speaks to the belief that something becomes lost in translation when messages and connections become mediated. By creating a "real-life" experience, the magazine promised to "transform the participants' experiences of being gay or homosexual into richer contexts wherein their lives can be lived in ways which are truly self-enhancing and contribute to all of society." (Watson 1977) This makes it clear that just connecting with others "virtually" or being informed is not enough to be respectable member of the LGBT*Q+ community. Instead, it requires those personal connections to be who you "should" be.

By identifying gay and lesbian businesses and establishments as well as gay- and lesbian- welcoming establishments, the classifieds provided another service to gay and lesbian individuals on top of providing ways to connect with one another. Speaking to the importance of promoting and supporting gay and lesbian businesses is the fact that in addition to the classified ads within, there were entire directories dedicated to listing these businesses. Resources such as *Bob Damron's Address Book* (later rebranded as *Damron's Travel Guide*) and *Gay and Lesbian Yellow Pages* (for a variety of cities) provided a directory to find businesses that were owned and operated by members of the LGBT*Q+ community. While this did include bars, clubs, and bathhouses for those new to the scene in that community or merely traveling through, these guides also contained ads for mundane companies and services such as cleaning and repair services and clothing stores. The message behind this is clear: to be a part of the gay community, one needs to be able to support others and help make the community self-sufficient. This emphasis on local connections became one of driving reasons behind the metropolis-centric views behind much of gay culture.

THE COMPUTER AGE

Mediated forms of making personal connections have been around within the LGBT*Q+ community since the advent of gay- and lesbian-specific periodicals, so it is not surprising that it did not take long to adopt computerized dating, with services such as DATAGAY, a San Francisco-based company that promised "a unique nationwide computerized introduction service" (DATAGAY 1979). The image in one ad shows an illustration of a young, fit, shirtless, white man straddling a computer stool looking at an image of a relatively young, white man with a mustache. Unlike the previous advertisements for services such as GSF, this ad features very little text and is much more image centric. One of the messages conveyed in this simple image, however, is who this service is designed and intended for—attractive white men. The other thing that becomes apparent is that while other services and even personal ads focused on finding people with similar interests and desires (after all, you had to connect with a person before you could even send or see a photo), this service placed a heavy emphasis on looks. You now not only had to have similar interests, but you also had to be aesthetically pleasing to even make a connection, a characteristic that had previously set classifieds and dating services apart from other fashions of meeting people such as cruising or in bars.

Further technological innovations led to another shift in the ways that LGBT*Q+ individuals were connecting with each other. With the adoption of personal computers and the Internet, gay- and lesbian-specific chat rooms and discussion boards became available to provide ways to chat with individuals both internationally and locally. Services such as CompuServe in the 1980s and later America Online offered easy access for anyone who had a dial-up Internet connection to instantly connect with others and even share photos (if one did not mind a 15-minute download time) (Auerbach and Prescott 2014; Grov et al. 2014; Tyrangiel 2000; Walker 2016). For the more technically savvy, there were also gay bulletin board services (BBSs), such as Backroom that would allow individuals to chat anonymously with others about politics, cruising locations, and fetishes, and even share porn (Auerbach and Prescott 2014).

Numerous other sites popped up, such as Adam4Adam, Gay.com, and Manhunt, that allowed men to meet other locals for dates, sexual encounters, friendships, and to just chat. While the sites geared toward men tended to focus on sexual encounters and interests (as was the case within many of the older forums for classified ads), there were also spaces created specifically for women. These spaces tended to be mailing lists with the purpose of communicating with other lesbian women, such as *Euro-Sappho* and *US-Sappho* lists (Auerbach and Prescott 2014; Isaksson 1997). These served as ways to forge romances and friendships, both locally and internationally.

Even though there were geographic-specific lists, numerous women were joining lists for other countries/continents. In a saved post from her *Euro-Sappho* account, Isaksson explains the ways in which women were networking across the globe.

> Some numbers: Of the 60 lists in the list of lesbian lists (in January 1997), 50 were running on U.S. servers. 55 of those 60 lists use English as their only or primary language. The first U.S. list started in 1987 and the first European list in 1993. Of the lesbian online population, approximately 9/10 or more are from North America.
>
> The main purpose of the first international European lesbian list, Euro-Sappho, was to serve as the home base for European lesbians and bisexual/queer women. Likewise, the wild-list for European lesbian studies started to facilitate networking and contacts between European women involved in lesbian and queer studies. Both of those lists have however been open to all women who have wanted to join.
>
> When Euro-Sappho was started in July 1994, a fairly considerable number of North Americans joined it at once. In the beginning, reaching out to more Europeans and to building the list into the European forum it became was slow work. When I looked at my archives, I found out that in mid-July 1994, there were 67 women subscribed to Euro-Sappho. 26 of them were from North American addresses, i.e. almost 40 percent. (Isaksson 1997)

Another one of the differences between the gay-specific sites and the lesbian-specific forms of online communication was the immediacy of expected meeting. While many of the sites for men were geared toward fast connections and sexual encounters, the mailing lists and connections available to women were often more relationship- and friendship-oriented and relationships would largely be developed online before ever meeting in person. One thing that was similar for both forms of communication, however, was that they provided individuals questioning their sexuality a place to explore and learn about LGBT*Q+ culture and terminology—a sentiment that came up in many of the interviews I conducted as well as in my own personal experiences.

Soon after these sites and lists became popular, other dating services (e.g., OKCupid) and posting sites (e.g., Craigslist) decided to become openly LGBT*Q+-friendly and offer additional services and features for them. This availability to connect within already popular, better advertised, and more mainstream websites began to make the LGBT*Q+-specific ones somewhat obsolete (Auerbach and Prescott 2014; Tyrangiel 2000; Walker 2016). One possibility of this is because it allowed a safer space for individuals who had not disclosed their SOGI since mere use of the site was not an indication of one's gender or sexual orientation.

AN EMPHASIS ON THE POLITICAL AND EDUCATIONAL

LGBT*Q+ media was not just for the sole purpose of forging connections and finding a community, it has also always been a venue for educating individuals about issues deemed important to the community. Since many gay and lesbian periodicals originated as methods of dissemination for various homophile groups, such as the Mattachine Society, it makes sense that at least the origins of LGBT*Q+ periodicals would have a heavy political emphasis. While the specific political aims of the publications varied, they did share a common sentiment in the notion that a queer population needed to be a politically active and educated population. LGBT*Q+ periodicals flourished in the 1970s amid backlash occurring against the LGBT*Q+ population in the wake of newly gained freedom from the 1969 riots and Gay Liberation Day marches of the early 1970s. One of the reasons for this was to keep many readers informed about timely and important issues. This was done with a deliberate attempt to educate those within (and outside of) the community about the history of LGBT*Q+ individuals throughout all cultures and time-periods. For example, a 2003 issue of *XY* magazine has an entire section dedicated to gay history tracing the time line back to 1200 BC, a trend that has continued to today with many online websites discussing homosexuality in ancient cultures.

Informational projects such as this work to serve two distinct purposes. The first is to engrain the idea of homosexuality throughout history in order to naturalize it, rather than to view it as a social construct that scholars like D'Emilio (1983) argue arose due to the conditions of capitalism and modernity. D'Emelio and others do not claim that same-sex attraction and activities did not take place prior to modernity, but rather that the notion of an LGBT*Q+ community and identity was formed due to the affordances and conditions offered by capitalism. The second function of these projects is to relate the stigmatization of LGBT*Q+ individuals with previous suffering and discrimination of gay and lesbian individuals, with ads drawing upon the pink triangle used to denote homosexuals within the Holocaust and comparing gay individuals with other refugees and oppressed minorities.

Many of the political articles were focused specifically on issues that would be affecting the LGBT*Q+ community at the time: potential legislation, lawsuits, discriminatory practices, etc. Among these types of stories/ resources provided was a heavy emphasis on health-related issues that disproportionately affected the LGBT*Q+ community. One of the issues that was tackled from early on was the increased rate of attempted suicide in LGBT*Q+ individuals relative to their straight counterparts. (Asala 2010; Carosone 2013; Remafedi, Farrow, and Deisher 1991) This was done in two main ways: 1) sharing pertinent information about the risk and 2) as an attempt to break the shame and silence that often accompanies suicide—both for those who have attempted and those who know individuals who have attempted.

This need to inform the LGBT*Q+ population of health-related issues only expounded during the 1980s at the onset of the GRID (Gay Related Immune Deficiency) crisis (later named AIDS or Acquired Immune Deficiency Syndrome). Numerous articles were published within various publications warning individuals of risk factors, as well as signs to look out for.

Since it could be easy for many to overlook reading articles that covered these health issues (they were not usually the most eye-catching visually), Eclipse Enterprises of Forestville, California began producing AIDS Awareness cards in 1993 to provide a more creative way to reach a larger audience. Initiated by a company that was primarily known to create comic books, these cards were a more creative attempt to reach a larger audience. Not without controversy, however, the cards also contained condoms and graphic images of how to use them, which worked to link AIDS predominantly with unsafe sexual practices, while obscuring other ways to contract the disease. Additionally, in spite of accusations these cards were "capitalizing on people's tragedy," the creators of the cards defended them by stating that those that took time to read all of the information would get a good understanding of the disease and the risks surrounding it (Robinson, n.d.). These cards contained information about famous individuals who had contracted HIV as well as prevention measures.

WE'RE HERE, WE'RE QUEER, GET USED TO IT

Outside of just sharing health-related information relevant to the LGBT*Q+ community, there has been one other prevailing topic that has permeated all forms of LGBT*Q+ media: the importance and political nature of coming out. From the pre-Stonewall days and the Mattachine Society and other organizers telling individuals that they needed to come out to increase visibility of the gay and lesbian population (D'Emilio 1998; Stewart-Winter 2016) to Harvey Milk's speeches urging every gay and lesbian man and woman to come out (Shilts 2008) to the anti-Prop 8 campaign in California in 2008 (A. B. Becker and Scheufele 2009), coming out has long been considered a political and *moral* imperative for the LGBT*Q+ community, and is viewed, as such, as a sort of ritual-based rite of passage.

It is through examining the idea of coming out through Foucault's discourse about confession that we can begin to see both the power that coming out can have for individuals, as well as the power exerted upon those individuals by society through forcing them to come out.

> The confession has spread its effects everywhere. It plays a part in justice, medicine, education, family relationships, and love relations, in the most ordi-

nary affairs of everyday life, and in the most solemn rites; one confesses one's
crimes, one's sins, one's thoughts and desires, one's illnesses and troubles; one
goes about telling, with the greatest precision whatever is most difficult to tell.
(1990, p. 59)

Foucault goes on to discuss the ways in which the act of confession can be a
freeing act (Foucault, 1990), much like the way that Milk described coming
out as having a liberatory power (Shilts, 2008). Taken literally, it could be
easy to dismiss Foucault's discussion of confession as referring only to a
Catholic priest, but what is underlying in all of this is that one confesses that
which is not normal. When someone's thoughts or actions conform to the
societal norms, there is no need to confess them to anyone as they are assumed; however, it is when they deviate from those norms that a confession
is mandated—by either the self, society, or both.

This notion that we need to confess the inner turmoil or differences that
we have has become a central component of the therapy culture that pervades
so much of United States popular culture (Bellah, 1996). "We have seen that
therapy has developed an acute concern for the monitoring and managing of
inner feelings and emphasizes their expression in open communication"
(Bellah, 1996, p. 138). This is something easy to see within our current
popular media environment with successful shows such as *Dr. Phil*, *Dr. Oz*,
The Doctors, and numerous others that all offer pop psychology advice about
how to get in touch with and express our feelings. It is not enough to become
merely comfortable with our feelings, but to be truly happy individuals, we
need to express these feelings to the world—which, in turn, needs to accept
us.

It is in this way that we can begin to understand that coming out is not
solely a political action as had once been called for by activists like Harvey
Milk (including more contemporary activist organizations during the recent
fights for marriage equality), but it is also something that is intensely personal and is considered an action that needs to be taken before one is able to be a
truly happy and authentic individual. In fact, in the LGBT*Q+ community
there is often a tendency to view those who have not come out, without
regard for reasons, as being less authentic or stunted in their development
(Adams, 2010; Rasmussen, 2004). This also tends to ignore the fact that there
are often cultural factors (such as ethnicity and religious beliefs) that seem to
play a large role on when one will come out and how one's coming out will
be received (Etengoff & Daiute, 2015; Grov, Bimbi, Nanin, & Parsons, 2006;
Ross, 2005). This push for individuals to come out and be "authentic" can
also create anxiety, with some individuals not feeling ready to come out or
choosing to delay for a variety of reasons, which do not include leading an
inauthentic existence, but rather merely reflect a complex set of conflicting
identities (Grov et al., 2006; Owens, 2015; Solomon et al., 2015).

One of the ways that this emphasis on coming out has happened on such a large scale is through the discussion about it within LGBT*Q+-centric media. Nearly every single archival publication that I examined for this study had at least one, if not numerous, issues that centered solely around the idea of coming out being a moral imperative in ways that created a binary between "good gays" and "bad gays." For instance, in a 1979 issue of *The Barb* an article titled "Laconic Commands" instructed LGBT*Q+ individuals with what they needed to do to be a good and contributing member to gay culture. Providing readers with a list of ten commandments, number seven is to "Come Out!" and advises people to come out to as many people as they can; other commands range from learning to love yourself to supporting gay businesses to being politically active. While it does mention that some people may not "feel" that they cannot come out completely, it segues into donating money to gay organizations if one cannot come out. In this way, the only "legitimate" reason for not coming out is due to the potential financial repercussions (perhaps of losing one's job). Moreover, there is only one acceptable way to be a member of the gay community according to this and anyone who does not follow these commandments becomes categorized as "less developed." While the final paragraph of this article tells the reader to follow the commandments that work for them, the final statement again makes it clear that by taking these actions it is you who will benefit through your own rights and freedoms.

It was not just *The Barb* that placed this huge emphasis on the need to come out. Numerous articles in a variety of periodicals painted similar pictures around coming out, many of them focusing on the necessity of it and providing tools and tips to help individuals get through this difficult time in life. The necessity to come out for both political gains and personal happiness, while gaining popularity in the late 1960s throughout the 1970s (although some homophile organizations had been calling for this since before the 1950s) has now become a staple of the modern LGBT*Q+ rights movement. In 2003, *XY* magazine created an entire issue dedicated to creating a "survival guide" to being gay, which involved entire sections dedicated to coming out, how to do it, and why it was necessary.

The argument from within the LGBT*Q+ community for the need to come out largely stems from the reality that SOGI are often invisible identity categories. Therefore, unless you tell people, they may not realize you are part of that group. However, due to the focus solely on SOGI, other important factors related to questions of identity can often be overlooked and become absorbed by the "default" of white maleness (Ahmed 2006; Crenshaw 1991; Puar 2007, 2012). Despite being considered a paragon of proper identity development within the LGBT*Q+ community, coming out has additional complications when questions of race, ethnicity, class, and religion are factored in that can all affect the ways that one's coming out is both realized internally and accepted externally (Etengoff and Daiute 2015; Gertler 2014; Grov et al. 2006). By centering on one monolithic notion of how and when one should come out, the most marginalized within the LGBT*Q+ community are further cast aside as whiteness, maleness, and middle-classness become centered as traits of the ideal queer individual.

CREATION/REINFORCEMENT OF STEREOTYPES

Perhaps one of the more lasting impacts of the topics covered and the images used, created, and spread throughout LGBT*Q+ periodicals is the creation of stereotypes as well as creating certain ideals of how gay male individuals are supposed to look and act. While modern media has expanded this to include stereotypes of lesbian, bisexual, and trans* individuals, throughout the periodicals I reviewed in this study, representations of women and trans* individuals were almost entirely absent. When lesbian women were included, the portrayals were significantly different than those of men and often focused on family, love, and political activism compared to portrayals of men, which emphasized physical attractiveness and sexual promiscuity. Representations of women were also often secluded into their own separate publications almost exclusively targeting lesbian women. *The Advocate*, for example, covered issues that allegedly spoke to the entire LGBT*Q+ community and often touted itself as a voice for all. Nevertheless, the majority of images in the issues examined were of men and were often very sexualized in nature. This erasure in and of itself is telling by showing the emphasis on gay men and how women and "gay rights" were often treated as separate entities. This division between gay men and the rest of the community will be explored in more depth later in this chapter in the section "Divisions Within." This section will be focusing on the messages created about gay men regarding sexual desire and desirability of different individuals.

It's Just Sex

Since many early social gatherings of gay men revolved around discreet sexual encounters, it is logical that there would be a heavy emphasis on sex, at least in the early days of these periodicals. Advertising throughout the 60s and 70s was very sexually explicit, regardless of message content (e.g., political messages). In a 1976 issue of *The Barb*, an article entitled "A Day with Sunshine" discusses the passage of an ordinance that would protect gay and lesbian individuals in Miami-Dade County; the article frames a large advertisement for the gay complex Parliament House (located in Orlando, FL) that is located in the middle of the page, almost as large as the text of the article. Using high-contrast black and white, the advertising features a fully naked man sitting on a cheetah-patterned blanket. Over this image, there is dark text providing information about the gay bar and hotel. However, because of the dark font color and the brightness of the white model (and the fact that the text is laid out so that it frames his penis) the model (and more specifically his penis) is where the eye is first drawn. Additionally, by juxtaposing this advertisement with an otherwise unrelated article, it implies that the two should be connected in some way. A careful reader of the article would understand it was applauding the passage of the ordinance and that it contained a critique of Anita Bryant; the casual reader would likely think it is an article merely promoting this venue.

Highly sexual advertisements are neither novel nor related only to the gay male population (Reichert and Lambiase 2003), but centering the majority of ads around companies featuring overtly sexual images when not related to sex (i.e., not for a bathhouse or pornography) did work to link gay sexual identity with promiscuity and partying. While stereotypes of highly promiscuous gay men are still prevalent, they no longer hold the same social status as they once did within the gay community (*Afro-American Red Star* 2001; Swain 2007). As the LGBT*Q+ community began to gain legal and social acceptance throughout the 1970s these sexual practices began to become ostracized within the community. Even before the AIDS epidemic became visible and understood, the ways that articles discussed public sex had started to change drastically, albeit not unproblematically. In a March 1980 issue of *The Advocate*, the cover page featured the headline "Tribal Rites of the Anonymous Bushman" in addition to several black-and-white photos and drawings of naked men (one man is fully clothed but has his trousers unzipped and his erect penis is exposed) standing in a lush green jungle. By placing these men within an overgrown jungle under the headline, this issue conjures up images of the numerous anthropological studies carried out in many colonized nations throughout the world, in which the "superior" Western scientist went to observe the "primitive" lifestyles of the indigenous peoples (Smith 2012).

The issue continues with the standard "Opening Space" in which the publisher of the paper habitually included a general letter to the public with his views on an important topic (typically related to the main stories of that issue). This particular editorial centers on the questions of sexual responsibility, how much sex is too much, and the image that we portray to the world. The main moral of the message is that individuals who focus their sexual identity mainly on sexual encounters are irresponsible and are doing a disservice to themselves and the community as a whole; it is more important to show the world that you are a productive and contributing member of society. In this way public sex is considered off limits to him and sex within back rooms is demeaning (but not unforgivably so) (Goodstein 1980). It is within this framing that the featured article of this issue is contextualized for the reader and given the title "Quick Encounters of the Closest Kind: The Bush

League—The Rites and Rituals of Shadow Sex" and focused on exploring the complicated world of gay cruising in a sex club, building on Humphrey's sociological study *Tearoom Trade*. The article then proceeds to relate the cruising culture to drug addicts before finally coming to the conclusion that it will never go away and seems to be a fundamental part of male sexuality (Willenbecher 1980).

Moving forward two years, AIDS had begun to affect the gay urban community and was creating panic among the community, and sexual promiscuity, particularly that within large metropolitan areas, became associated with both an outdated lifestyle and with new dangers. The month after featuring an article asking whether sex was dangerous for the urban gay male, *The Advocate* featured another issue exploring urban male sexuality with the title "Manhattan Hunting Grounds," featuring an image on the cover of the door to a seedy men's bathroom presumably in the subway system of New York City. What follows are two side-by-side articles (placed top to bottom on the pages) that span 7 pages each: the top article entitled "Manhattan Hunting Grounds" and the bottom "The Synagogue, The Saint and the Mine Shaft."

Centered on the first page between these two articles is a black-and-white photo of a man in a trench coat standing at a urinal in the middle of a dilapidated public bathroom. The first article functions as an educational tool in helping the audience understand cruising culture and the second functions as a reminiscing of the lost Gemeinschaft of the past gay community in the wake of the new Gesellschaft of sexual liberation, increased social acceptance, and new and dangerous diseases (Tönnies 2002). Both articles are followed by another article, "A Scholarly Taxi to the Toilets," that features an interview with scholar Humphreys about his work on gay cruising culture. The article concludes with the fact that this activity should be abandoned in favor of safer and more "prideful" sexual encounters. Interestingly the other featured article within the section highlights the lesbian experience in Chicago. Contrasting the portrayal of the sexual habits of gay men, the article on the women in Chicago portrays a diverse group of women who focus largely on issues of social justice and efforts to create a diverse and changing community.

This distinction between different types of sexual activities and practices becomes important as it laid one of the foundations for differentiating between "good gays" and "bad gays," a stereotype that exists to this day. According to Henderson (2013), promiscuity and being unable to hamper one's sexual desire often results in them being categorized as a bad gay, whereas good gays engage in a more limited, respectable type of sexual behavior. This split serves as one of the factors that has led to divisions and discriminations within the LGBT*Q+ community, a topic that will be discussed more fully in the next section of this chapter.

Let's Get Physical

In 1978, the iconic gay group the Village People released their hit single, "Macho Man," featuring the following lyrics:

Every man wants to be a macho man
To have the kind of body always in demand

While now an often-parodied song, it does speak to what had become portrayed as the ideal body and personality types for gay men: muscular and masculine. While not explicitly stated within many articles, images in both articles and advertisements provide a clear indication of what comprised the "attractive" gay man. Even though there was some (albeit limited) visibility for gay men of color in groups such as the Village People, similar to the lack of women and trans* individuals, there was an overall lack of representation for men of color and skinny, overweight, disabled, or feminine men in most gay imagery. While larger publications like *The Advocate* would occasionally publish articles that dealt with an issue related to one of these groups, most of these articles were almost always centered on the differences from those individuals and the "rest" of the community. Representations of gay people of color were (and still are) often in magazines or clubs targeting those groups or as part of an evening that fetishizes certain groups.

Understandably, having separate channels of representation specifically for groups that are historically underrepresented is not problematic, but the notion that those venues are specialized parties or publications while those that feature issues related to and images of predominantly white men are viewed as "standard" ones is problematic. Additionally, there appears to be a continued divide between masculine and feminine traits even within these specialized publications. The 2011 swimsuit issue of *Swerv* magazine, geared toward the African American LGBT*Q+ community within the United States, featured two different covers. In comparison to such magazines as *Sports Illustrated*, which has consistently had different models on different covers of their swimsuit issues, *Swerv* has two strikingly different versions of their cover.

One of the covers features a heavily muscled black man clad in leather and chains wearing sunglasses. The text is a crisp white, and the model fills up almost the entire frame, even blocking the "e" in *Swerv* with their head. They are leaning up against a plain, dark gray background with nothing else in the frame other than a glimpse of the stool he was leaning on. The other image, however, features a light-skinned, very feminine person wearing a bright pink one-piece bathing suit, large earrings, a scarf, and bangles. They are standing in front of a wall that is adorned with ivory and, compared with the other cover, appears diminutive in the frame, with their big hairpiece not even nearing the top of the frame. Another distinct feature is that the majority of the font on this second image is a bright pink matching the swimsuit the model is wearing. Additionally, while the model in leather seems to be staring straight at us (it is hard to tell for sure with the sunglasses), the one in pink is staring off to the side seemingly unaware that they are subject to the audience's gaze. These two covers provide a clear indication of what traits are more respected within this community—masculinity and muscularity.

Divisions Within

Despite often being described as a monolithic culture or group, the LGBT*Q+ community has historically been anything but unified regarding acceptance of diversity within. Much of this is enabled through media representations of LGBT*Q+ individuals, both historically and contemporary, as well as within both mainstream and LGBT*Q+ media outlets.

The Stonewall Riots began through the combined work of lesbians, transgender women, drag queens, and gay men (of all races and ethnicities). Regardless of this, it did not take long before the gay men (specifically gay white men) began to distance themselves from those they found to be "sissies" or harmful or irrelevant to their agenda. This was done in a variety of ways throughout the media, including both a lack of representation and a purposeful exclusion. One of the groups that was very directly excluded was women. Most of representations were (and largely still are) of white, muscular men focused mainly on attracting male clients.

When women were represented within news outlets that were not specifically just for lesbians, there was backlash and resentment from within the gay, male community as one letter to the editor pointed out within a 1978 issue of *The Advocate*:

> I resent strongly being forced to read lesbian news which you have incorporated within The ADVOCATE. While cramming lesbianism down the readers' throat may make you richer, I for one won't continue to read The ADVOCATE. I find it distasteful. The least you could do is put the lesbian news in one fold-out section. As a homosexual I consider what you are doing no better than what the heterosexuals do by attempting to indirectly force their lifestyle on everybody. (Name withheld 1978)

Indeed, this is not necessarily representative of the majority of individuals within the LGBT*Q+ community. Nonetheless, this letter does speak to a divide that has existed within media between gay men and women and continues to exist to this day (Jotanovic 2017).

In 2015, Roland Emmerich directed the film *Stonewall*, a semi-fictional story depicting the birth of the LGBT*Q+ rights movement during the Stonewall Riots. The movie created a fictional character of Danny as the main character who the film follows and who ultimately starts the riots. Danny is the epitome of white, cis-male privilege who, according to Emmerich was created in order to provide a window into the LGBT*Q+ community (Ginelle 2015; Ramirez 2015). The film follows Danny as he moves from Indiana to New York City after being disowned by his family, something that has been considered almost a gay imperative.

Even though gay sex has been continuously present in all areas of the country throughout history, there existed a presumed notion during this era of the 70s and 80s that those who did not live in a major city such as New York, Los Angeles, Chicago, or San Francisco were oppressed and thus were somewhat stunted within their gay development (Herring 2010; Howard 2001). This sentiment is expressed throughout many of the articles throughout the 1970s and 1980s, not always overtly but usually subtly. For instance, in the "Laconic Commands" article from *The Barb* previously discussed in this chapter there is never a command that one must move to a city, but many of the commands (such as "support gay businesses") require one to live within a gay ghetto. A 1970s issue of *Come Out!* (produced by the Gay Liberation Front) included a supplement that discussed the idea of gay liberation that contained a "gay manifesto" that spoke of the importance of having gay ghettos and stated that San Francisco had become a gay refuge.

These factors combined began to make a very clear gay ideal, achievable by white, cisgender, masculine men while others were purposefully excluded through the guise of sexual "preferences." Within personal ads placed in newspapers, phrases like "no S/M [sadomasochism], fats, fems [*sic*], or weirdos," "white male. . . . looking for sincere friend and companionship for sex with other white male," and "seeking lover. Must be white, to early 30's, m about 6,' masculine, muscular" were commonplace. These individuals desired the models they saw in the ads because that was how desirability in the gay community became branded. This is not to state this was accepted by all, and it was frequently challenged throughout many different publications as critiquing the "clones"—those who tried to live the epitome of what they saw in the advertisements as "gay culture." In 1984, Howard Cruse and Roberta Gregory published an issue of *Gay Comix* that featured a strip entitled "Cabbage Patch Clone" which follows an attractive, white, masculine man who orders one of these dolls. When the doll is just there for his pleasure, he enjoys it; eventually the doll begins to talk, thus making the relationship complicated and resulting in the man kicking the doll out the window.

A more direct critique of representation and privileging certain bodies over others came in a 1995 issue of *The Advocate* that featured a three-page advertisement critiquing the images prevalent within gay advertising. The advertisement starts out by stating "A very special gay pride message brought to you by your community's publishers, advertisers, merchants, clothiers, and club owners" and then directs the reader to turn the page. On the next page is a collage of images of white, muscular, naked men around the text "If you don't look like the men on these pages . . . you're a worthless piece of shit." The next page features more similar images and includes a "post" from a message board online showcasing the high priority of looks within the gay community.

From the early days of the homophile movements, the LGBT*Q+ population has used media to help form communities. This has had both positive and negative cultural remnants of the LGBT*Q+ community to this day. Since LGBT*Q+ publications primarily began as organizational newsletters, it is important to understand that consistently politics and education about LGBT*Q+ history have been at the core of LGBT*Q+ publications. In addition to politics, forming personal connections with others has been central to the mission of LGBT*Q+ periodicals. One of these political messages has been about the importance of coming out. Coming out has often been viewed as a LGBT*Q+ imperative; this was the case since before Stonewall, and the media has placed a high priority and high visibility on this action. It has been necessary to live a legitimate LGBT*Q+ lifestyle and not be viewed as being repressed or underdeveloped. However, many of these narratives have been framed around the white, cisgender, and masculine experience in a way that obscures difference within the LGBT*Q+ community and oppresses those who do not fit the dominant narratives.

NOTES

1. The Lavender Scare refers to the persecution of individuals suspected of being homosexual during the Cold War, in which it was believed that homosexual individuals working in the government would be prime targets for Russian coercion.

2. For simplicity, all types of publications examined in these archives, when spoken about in general, will be referred to as periodicals. For specificity, it should be noted that these collections contained a variety of magazines, newspapers, zines, flyers, advertisements, posters, photographs, comic books, trading cards, and announcements for meetings. When discussing an individual example, the specific type of media artifact will be clearly denoted.

Chapter Three

Testing the Waters

Coming Out in a Hypermediated Age

Coming out has long held a central prominence within the LGBT*Q+ rights movement, as discussed within the previous chapter. Politics was often an underlying (or even overt) reason for LGBT*Q+ people to come out to those that they know. One of the other messages that has been at the heart of the push for individuals to come out is the idea that things will be better for you afterward. I know this was what I had heard when I was struggling with coming out, and while in some respects it does get better, there are also many times when other aspects of your life can become worse. I was fortunate that when I did eventually come out (albeit later in life) I had an accepting group of friends and family; however, that is not the case for many people—including several of those who I interviewed for this project.

When a young person is grappling with their sexuality, it is a particularly nerve-racking and confusing time in their life, with individuals usually starting to experience these sexual feelings as young as thirteen, but usually not coming to accept their sexual orientation until many years later (Grov et al. 2006). While general acceptance in the United States for LGBT*Q+ individuals has grown over the past several decades, there are still many LGBT*Q+ individuals who are grappling with this—many of whom face the very real threat of violence and bullying due solely to their sexual orientation (Owens 2015). Despite this, or perhaps in an attempt to combat this, there has been a growing trend of individuals coming out at younger ages (Goodman 2013). Nevertheless, this declaration of sexual orientation is still not a guarantee of a positive or accepting experience (Solomon et al. 2015).

In light of the potential turmoil, negative consequences, and anxiety that can fill this process of coming out, there has been an increase in generativity in recent years from those who have already come out as LGBT*Q+ to help others who are struggling with doing the same, which led to the now famous "It Gets Better" (IGB) campaign (Savage and Miller 2012). IGB consisted of individuals sharing their stories about how life improved for them after coming out. This was done with the intent to provide encouragement for teenagers contemplating suicide thinking that the bullying or stigma they were currently facing would follow them for the rest of their lives. This inspired another form of sharing, which became a lot more personal. Rather than merely describing their experiences during and after coming out, individuals started setting up cameras to candidly record themselves coming out "live" to their family members, which they then share through social media, especially through the video sharing site YouTube. This is, at least partially, to help others who might be struggling to do the same thing; it is also possible, though, that this is just the latest step for attention from a society that values the drama of reality television and "self-help" talk shows as popular forms of entertainment.

PHASES OF COMING OUT

Coming-out stories have become a staple within films and television shows that deal with LGBT*Q+ characters, to the point that they have become prioritized over any other type of story (Henderson 2013a). While indeed a historically and politically significant aspect of LGBT*Q+ culture, unfortunately, the emphasis on coming out can become problematic for several reasons. The first is that the issues and concerns surrounding one's coming out are not universal, with those individuals who were raised in a strict religious environment or part of an already marginalized racial or ethnic group reporting more difficulty with coming out and acceptance (Etengoff and Daiute 2015; Grov et al. 2006). This was an issue that arose in many of my interviews with the participants raised in a religious environment and/or those who were part of an ethnic or racial minority.

One of the other issues in the way that coming out is often described or shown is that it creates a dichotomy—one is either in or they are out. It is often framed as a singular moment, usually when one reveals their SOGI to their parents. Often after that moment one is "out" whereas before one is "in the closet"—independent of the number of individuals to whom they have disclosed this information. This becomes problematic in the sense that the actual reality of coming out becomes obscured by implying that there is ever such a thing as being completely "out." Rather than being a sole, defining moment that separates those who are out and those who are not (often regarded as being socially stunted, as previously discussed), coming out is a continual process that never truly ends for the entirety of one's life. This may get easier the more comfortable one gets with their own SOGI, but it is still a fact that when one meets someone for the first time, one's membership in the LGBT*Q+ community is not a known fact; moreover, it is a fact that the individual may choose not to disclose given its potentially negative ramifications.

Social media, considering its ability to connect us with others in faster and more pervasive ways than ever before, is amplifying this conundrum that LGBT*Q+ individuals face. Now, every single friend request and post becomes a potential way to come out to a new person. In this way one is never fully out, but rather being LGBT*Q+ is a process of continually coming out. With the prevalence and importance of social media within today's society, each post and privacy setting become a potential way to out oneself to someone new. In one way, this is helpful in that the "outing" can occur before one even meets someone or can help to aid in creating a mass coming out, as some of my participants utilized Facebook to do. Alternatively, as some of my participants experienced, it opens new ways to accidentally out oneself to unintended audiences.

Given these reasons, one of the arguments that I intend to put forth is that we must conceive of coming out as a continual process, rather than a single event. Additionally, we need to conceptualize it beginning earlier than traditionally perceived (disclosing one's SOGI to family or close friends); the process begins when individuals first come out to themselves. In every interview I conducted, respondents discussed how this was an initial hurdle of varying difficulty However, for most, social media proved to be an important and contributing factor to this self-revelation—a topic explored later in this chapter.

I conducted the interviews in two phases. The first was to engage in a casual conversation with each participant about their social media usage and their SOGI. Second, I followed up with a semi-structured interview in which I had each person vividly describe their coming-out experience in a detailed manner, from the moments immediately preceding that instant up through the present day. The questions focused on their feelings and emotional experience during the time, rather than just factual accounts of their coming-out experiences. In addition to their coming-out experience, we discussed media usage (both traditional and social/digital) at each stage of coming out. I prompted individuals to "Tell me about when [they] first realized that [they] were gay, lesbian, or bisexual." Later in the interview, I asked participants to "Tell me about when [they] came out for the first time." While seemingly straight forward questions, they proved rather difficult to answer; this was particularly true for gay men and for the first question.

One of the obvious reasons for this difficulty is the time that had lapsed since this realization occurred to present day—even for those individuals who recently came out to anyone. Individuals commonly answered by explaining how reflectively they can now see signs of their SOGI at a very young age.

COMING OUT AS THERAPEUTIC CONFESSION

Before fully delving into the role of social media in the coming-out process, it is important to examine the theoretical frameworks that can help us understand the coming-out process in general. The previous chapter outlined the history of how coming out developed into a political action in the late twentieth century, but the idea of coming out has roots dating much further back, arguably to the Catholic ritual of the confession. Additionally, Catholic confession has had a long history pertaining to sexuality. It is through examining the idea of coming out through Foucault's discourse about confession that we can begin to see both the power that coming out can have for individuals, as well as the power exerted by society upon those individuals by forcing them to come out. The confession has spread its effects far and wide. It plays a part in justice, medicine, education, family relationships, and love relations, in the most ordinary affairs of everyday life, and in the most solemn rites; one confesses one's crimes, one's sins, one's thoughts and desires, one's illnesses and troubles; one goes about telling, with the greatest precision, whatever is most difficult to tell (Foucault 1990, 59).

Foucault goes on to discuss the ways in which the act of confession can be a freeing act (Foucault 1990), much like the way that Milk described coming out as having a liberatory power. Taken literally, it could be easy to dismiss Foucault's discussion of confession as referring only to a Catholic priest, but what is underlying in all of this is that one confesses that which is not normal. When someone's thoughts or actions conform to the societal norms, there is no need to confess them to anyone as they are assumed; it is when they deviate from those norms that a confession is mandated—either by the self, society, or both.

This notion that we need to confess the inner turmoil or differences that we have has become a central component of the therapeutic culture that pervades so much of US popular culture (Bellah 1996). "We have seen that therapy has developed an acute concern for the monitoring and managing of inner feelings and emphasizes their expression in open communication" (Bellah 1996, 138). This is something easy to see within our current popular media environment with such successful shows such as *Dr. Phil*, *Dr. Oz*, and *The Doctors* (just to name a few) that offer pop psychology advice about how to get in touch with and express our feelings. It is not enough to become comfortable with our feelings—in order to be truly happy individuals, we need to express these feelings to the world, which, in turn, needs to accept us for these to respect our individuality.

There is a tension that exists between the supposedly liberatory act of openly expressing one's SOGI to the world and the fact that this declaration is only forced upon those who do not confine to the cisgender, heteronormative expectations placed upon them by society. Most of the individuals I interviewed expressed this ambivalence. In some regards, they described the moments after coming out as cathartic (particularly those who had recently come out). Alternatively, although not always clearly expressed, there was a sense of othering that everyone felt, due to the demand placed upon them to come out. It became clear that while clearly having personal liberatory potential, because of assumed reality of proscribed compulsory heterosexuality (Ahmed 2006) that the coming-out process still functions in order to separate LGBT*Q+ individuals from their "normal" counterparts (Foucault 1990). Coming out is, therefore, almost exclusively discussed regarding its potential for liberation, while ignoring the complex societal structures that it serves to reinforce.

It is in this way that we can begin to understand that coming out is not solely a political action as once called for by activists like Harvey Milk (including more contemporary activist organizations during the recent fight for marriage equality), but it by virtue an intensely personal action crucial for being truly happy and authentic. This tends to ignore the fact that there are cultural factors (such as ethnicity and religious beliefs) that play a significant role in both the coming-out time line and reception of such (Etengoff and Daiute 2015; Grov et al. 2006). This push for individuals to come out and be "authentic" can also create anxiety, with some individuals not feeling ready to come out or choosing to delay for a variety of reasons, often related to a complex set of conflicting identities (Grov et al. 2006; Owens 2015; Solomon et al. 2015).

Despite an increase in visibility from people listening to the calls of leaders of the LGBT*Q+ rights movement throughout the 1970s, times only became more challenging for gay men when the AIDS epidemic erupted in the 1980s. President William H. Clinton eventually signed several acts into law: Don't Ask Don't Tell and the Defense of Marriage Act. These laws helped to solidify LGBT*Q+ individuals as second-class citizens and would remain as laws until 2010 and 2013, respectively. Additionally, the bullying of LGBT*Q+ youth continues to be a problem, resulting in high rates of suicide for this population due to the hopelessness that many of them feel (Remafedi et al., 1991).

In direct response to the crisis concerning these high rates of suicide due to bullying for LGBT*Q+ youth, columnist Dan Savage and his partner, Terry Miller, created a video about their coming out in 2010 that they uploaded to YouTube. The intent was to preach their message that the bullying will not last, and that life will get better, because, according to Savage "all of the gay, lesbian, bisexual, and transgender adults [he] knew were leading rich and rewarding lives" (Savage and Miller 2012, 3). Savage describes in his book that he felt compelled to do something about this latest tragedy to strike the LGBT*Q+ community, and it was through the affordances of YouTube that he was able to reach a large audience and launch a massive campaign that has resulted in hundreds of shared videos, all of people telling their stories of how "things got better." In the meantime, while we work to make our schools safer, we can and should use the tools we have at our disposal right now—social media and YouTube and this book—to get messages of hope to kids who are suffering right now in schools that do not have GSAs and to kids whose parents bully and reject them for being lesbian, gay, bisexual, or transgender. (Savage and Miller 2012, 7)

That is not to say that IGB is without fault, as it has fallen under a lot of criticism for focusing only on a few types of stories, while possibly further marginalizing other groups (Wight 2014). Despite some of its flaws, it is still generally seen as a positive step forward in helping to intervene in the lives of these at-risk youth (Goltz 2013). This mediated generativity in which LGBT*Q+ individuals who grew up feeling isolated wish to act as positive role models for others who may be feeling the same way, regardless of interpersonal familiarity (Goltz 2013), has recently taken on a new form in individuals setting up (usually) hidden cameras to capture their actual coming-out experience on video to share with others through social networking sites. These "live" coming-out videos both spread awareness and sensitivity to LGBT*Q+ issues, as well as reinforce specific heteronormative and neoliberal values and beliefs.

COMING OUT AND MEDIA REPRESENTATIONS

Videos depicting candid moments of coming out also function as models for individuals who are deciding whether to come out in a way that allows them to experience the process firsthand before committing to their own version of the process. While this is not new to social media and coming-out stories have existed within media for a while (e.g., "The Puppy Episode" from *Ellen* in 1997 when her character came out) (Becker 2006) the realness purported by these videos has added an additional element of authenticity to viewers to help offer them hope. This is not to state that one venue of representation takes priority or is more effective or useful than the others. However, based on the interviews with my participants, they do have different uses— traditional media was good for gauging others' opinions and digital/new media was good for gaining confidence and a sense of identity.

One of the most recurring themes throughout all the interviews was the notion that popular media representations were useful for two reasons. The first was that these representations reduced a sense of exclusion and often became some of the first positive exposures to LGBT*Q+ individuals. This concept is not really anything new, but does speak to the importance that representation has for individuals who have historically been underrepresented. Almost all people I spoke with were coming to realize their sexual or gender identities within the 1990s or early 2000s, a period of time of increased representation of LGBT*Q+ individuals within mainstream television shows (Becker 2006). More than just providing a sense of belonging or understanding, another empowering usage of these television shows and movies was that it gave a safe way for individuals to test out the reactions or opinions of their families before deciding whether to come out.

As popular media representations of LGBT*Q+ individuals became increasingly common throughout the 90s and into the 2000s, the ability to discuss, or even co-view, shows that featured LGBT*Q+ characters and dealt with issues for the LGBT*Q+ community became much easier. I remember in 2005, before I was out to family or friends, being able to discuss *Brokeback Mountain* with people helped me gauge how they felt about gay people in a way that felt safe and did not out myself. Not only was this an issue with face-to-face conversations, but posting about LGBT*Q+-related media or issues became an area of concern for individuals engaging with social media—an issue discussed in greater length in a later section in this chapter.

FINDING ONESELF ONLINE

In thinking of the impact that social media and the Internet have had on the coming-out process, the leading factor has arguably been the ability for individuals to find information and connect with other LGBT*Q+ individuals. Throughout my interviews, one of the most prevalent themes was the power of media (in a variety of forms) in the initial coming-out phase—when they came out to themselves. While many of the gay men I interviewed discussed the importance of mainstream representations of gay men in shows such as *Queer as Folk*, *Will & Grace*, and *Queer Eye for the Straight Guy*, many others expressed the importance of social media and the Internet in learning to understand their identity. Particularly for those with non-cisgender identities or those who did not fall neatly into either side of the perceived homo-/heterosexual dichotomy, the Internet, and particularly being able to talk with others who identified similarly to them, become a paramount and elucidating experience for them. Gemma, who identifies as an asexual, biromantic, cisgender woman, explained how it was through social media that she learned about asexuality:

> I actually learned about the term asexuality from Tumblr. It's not something that's very well known, even within the LGBT*Q+ community. And when it is it is often excluded. I found the term probably when I was around 16 or 17.

And it ate at my mind long enough so I finally googled it. And I found one of the main resource sites: The Asexual Visibility and Education Network. And so, on that, I found a forum and I found someone who was active on that forum and I started messaging her and asked about her experiences. This was when I was still trying to figure out if the term was right for me. Because, one of the hardest things I've found among other Ace people I've met is that it is really hard to determine if you are asexual when you've never known sexual attraction . . . you wonder "have I felt it and don't know it?" (personal communication, January 29, 2018)

Avery, who identifies as nonbinary and pansexual, also explained the importance of being able to connect with others through social media:

When I started to basically only use Twitter when I had moved home and was feeling very alone, I ended up connecting with people online. Most of whom were some flavor of trans* or something. A lot of us figured out in time, a lot of us who thought we were cisgender figured out. We learned a lot of different terms. I was probably identifying as non-binary about a year into that. (personal communication, January 30, 2018)

The one thing in common between all these different experiences is that it was only through having access to talk with, and learn from, others within the LGBT*Q+ community not afforded the same representation as others that they were able to start to understand their own feelings and life experiences. After benefiting from these groups, these individuals then joined in or started their own groups/forms of outreach to help others like themselves, illustrating Bellah's observation about how:

The therapeutic conception of community grows out of an old strand of American culture that sees social life as an arrangement for the fulfillment of the needs of individuals. In a "community of interest," self-interested individuals join together to maximize individual good. (1996, 134)

Belonging to these groups not only helped to create an understanding of self, but also an understanding of a sense of community. While seeking out these forums and groups was common among the trans*, poly, and asexual individuals that I spoke with, it was not the case with the gay and lesbian men and women who often cited becoming aware of their identity first through mainstream media before exploring gay and lesbian spaces online.

The one online resource that did come up as being an early source of educational and explorational material for young gay men was online pornography. This was not discussed in many of the interviews at great length (except for three individuals who spoke about it quite frankly), but was often hinted at, usually toward the very end of the interviews and observations. Those who did discuss it, expressed how access to free pornography on the

Internet became a learning moment about what being gay meant to them. This often was relevant in determining sexual preferences and the types of guys (and sex) in which the individual became interested. For example, Sean, who is Asian American and identifies as a gay, cisgender male, expressed how pornography and parties were his first conscious forays into gay culture and was likely one of the notable reasons that led to him finding bears[1] attractive.

> That was more a lot online. The random porn. This was more in high school. So, it was more finding online stuff. The 90s was when it started, when the whole bear culture started. I remember the International Bear Conference (IBC) and . . . websites would just have it. Like Shutterbear would go to all the, kind of, social group stuff and post all of that online. So that's where all the online stuff is where I started to get into that. And just as in high school, I noticed the more burly guys more . . . the wrestlers, you know the football players. Along with all of the interest online sparked all of that. That, and it was the same, I didn't want to be the typical type. I had seen all the . . . the *Queer as Folk* and everything else, because I wasn't ready to come out at that point. All of that influence was, "Oh god, oh god . . . If I'm interested in that . . . if I'm going with that . . . that means I'm gay." So in the sexual development, I was looking for everything that was the exact opposite of that. (personal communication, March 22, 2018)

While it makes sense that since the realization of one being gay often arises as one approaches puberty (and thus an awakening sexual attraction), the fact that pornography viewed at a young age features so prevalently into future sexual attraction is important to consider. It also speaks to a different way that individuals can find information and connections through social media based on their gender or sexual identity. While this is not to suggest a lack of non-pornographic or nonsexual social media sites for gay men, those sexual ones far outnumber the nonsexual ones. In fact, even sites such as Tumblr, Facebook, and Instagram, which almost every participant cited using, have distinct purposes for different people and often used by gay men for some type of sexual purpose. Tumblr was often cited, albeit reluctantly, as being used for free pornography—particularly when searching for certain fetishes that may not be represented within a lot of pornographic sites.

Although pornography could seem trivial to some, the enlightening factor of pornography for young gay men has not functioned substantially different than the way others were using chat rooms, bulletin board services, and discussion threads—they worked to provide a common language and vocabulary. While popular media did work to help some people's realization of their SOGI (mostly sexual), it was largely upon having private, heterotopic spaces away from the rest of (hetero-cis) society that allowed for a free and open space for individuals to explore their own identity when they were unsure how they fit within the larger society. Foucault referred to these spaces as crisis heterotopias—"privileged or sacred or forbidden places, reserved for individuals who are, in relation to society and to the human environment in which they live, in a state of crisis" (1984, 4). While Foucault felt that these spaces were disappearing, it is clear to me that in the digital world, at least for LGBT*Q+ individuals, they are thriving as spaces, unbound by geography providing refuge for those who feel as outcasts from the rest of society.

OF QUEER SPACES AND VOCABULARY

A recurring key theme throughout my interviews was the importance of having "safe" spaces of self-discovery. While there have long been ways for LGBT*Q+ individuals to meet with others like themselves (e.g., bars, bathhouses, private gatherings, political organizing, etc.), ripping these spaces from the constraints of geography provides an extra level of security for those individuals who are questioning their fit within society. Queer spaces surely contain some element of risk involved, however; for instance, while gay bars provided a secure place for queer individuals to meet, they were often also constantly at risk for being raided by police, which contained the very real risk of a public outing. If you were lucky enough not to be in the bar when the police raided it, there still existed the risk of being spotted when walking into the bar or related space. Digital spaces reduce (although not eliminate) the risk of accidental or unintentional outing, since they occur virtually and in the privacy of one's own home.

These spaces function for two main reasons. First, they provide a space and a sense of belonging with social support. Suicide attempts among LGBT*Q+ youth are very high compared with other youth demographics, and one of the biggest risk factors associated with this is a sense of social isolation (Remafedi, Farrow, and Deisher 1991). This holds especially true for individuals who are gender nonconforming, since that often increases a sense of difference among peers (Remafedi, Farrow, and Deisher 1991). During a time of isolation, bullying, and harassment, these digital heterotopias can offer a place of acceptance and inclusion. Cameron, who identifies as a queer heteroflexible, trans* man, explained how having these safe spaces online saved his life:

> I guess my first experience with social media would be YouTube. When I was 14 years old, I discovered YouTube was starting to become a bit bigger at that point and time, started to kind of takeoff. And that is when I started watching videos of other queer people. Even though queer wasn't even really a word that we used then . . . this was probably around 2008 or 2009. I came across a video of this guy that I was subscribed to and it was "What is the T in

LGBT*Q" and that is when I learned the word transgender for the first time. I had heard the terms transvestite, transsexual, cross-dresser, tranny, shit like that growing up . . . and at that point on I realized what the hell I was. I grew up very confused, isolated, paranoid, didn't really have a word for it, and then I was like . . . it just hit me like a ton of bricks. I didn't have to think twice about it. I was like, damn. And from there I kind of used YouTube to post my own content. Creating videos, a collaboration channel with other trans* teenagers. We kind of posted on trans* issues, topics. Through there I was able to form meetups, like in real life . . . and now I don't make YouTube videos anymore. Most of them are just private only I can see them . . . I'm trying to tip-toe the line of whether or not I want to be stealth. . . . If it wasn't for social media I don't know if I would be sitting here today. I don't know if I would be alive. The fact that I was able to get on the Internet and find that there were other people out there like me, saved my life completely. (personal communication, January 31, 2018)

More than just providing spaces to talk with other LGBT*Q+ individuals, through mediums such as YouTube, these heterotopias also provided forums for queer people to proselytize messages of love and acceptance, as well as to share their own stories.

While there is not one specific type of video that exists, one of the most powerful ones that my interviewees spoke about was candid coming-out videos. While the standard testimonial videos as offered by campaigns such as IGB were also discussed as helpful, these candid coming-out videos were often referred to as being more authentic and real, and thus resonating more with people. Since these videos were so influential among those I spoke with, it seems necessary to examine the work that they are doing in more detail, particularly the expectations that they set up and reinforce about the coming-out process.

COMING OUT LIVE

One of the driving factors for Savage to create his YouTube video was that he did not necessitate specific permissions from parents or educators to reach out to these kids—a permission that he felt would never be granted if requested.

In the era of social media—in a world with YouTube and Twitter and Facebook—I could speak directly to LGBT*Q+ kids now. I didn't need permission from parents or an invitation from a school. I could look into a camera, share my story, and let LGBT*Q+ kids know that it got better for me and it would get better for them too. I could give 'em hope. (Savage and Miller 2012, 4)

These affordances offered by the technologies readily available form a relatively low barrier to enter the world of video production on YouTube—one only needs access to a high-speed Internet connection and a computer or a smartphone. This provides access for numerous individuals to share their stories on YouTube and, by extension, much of the Internet, as the content uploaded to YouTube frequently is spread to other sites (e.g., Facebook, blogs) where others can interact with it in ways previously unavailable through interpersonal communication alone (Jenkins 2008). As discussed earlier, this is exactly what has been occurring within LGBT*Q+ youth and young adults, as they are no longer sharing their stories and messages of hope (a sentiment called for by both Milk and Savage), but rather are recording their actual coming-out experience and uploading it for thousands to view and discuss. This is in part functioning in a way to brand themselves in order to, according to Sarah Banet-Weiser (2011, 278), "communicate personal values, ideas, and beliefs using strategies and logic from consumer culture, and one that is increasingly normative in the contemporary neoliberal environment."

Often these videos use the descriptor "coming out live," and claim to capture, usually using a hidden camera, the moment that these individuals come out to a family member. It is interesting to note that none of the videos that I observed (twelve different individuals coming out and fourteen videos total) constituted the first coming out of an individual, but often usually was the first time they came out to a family member, with them having come out to one or two friends prior to this recording.

To purposively mimic the browsing that one might do when searching for videos to watch, I used the search terms "Coming Out Live" in YouTube's search feature and then used the autoplay feature to choose the other videos to be included in my analysis. This resulted in twelve different videos for a total of around 190 minutes of footage. Additionally, I did no research on the individuals who uploaded these videos to determine any cultural factors that may influence the content of the video. My justification for this is that I aimed to understand what images and icons circulate in the culture regarding the coming-out experience, particularly those that may be perceived as being authentic representations of this practice, as is the case in these videos. While the background of the individuals making these videos may play a role in the way that person chose to come out, it does not impact the way the audience will decode these videos. Notably, no other search terms (e.g., gay, lesbian, transgender, bisexual) were added that would potentially unnecessarily narrow or refine the search further. This searching method resulted in a prominent majority of videos representing cisgender, white men coming out as gay; the remaining videos consisted of one woman coming out to her grandparents as a lesbian, and two transgender individuals (one male to female [MTF] and the other one female to male [FTM]) coming out to their mother and sister, respectively. While it is theoretically possible that different search terms would have resulted in different videos to surface, it is important to examine the location and accessibility of these coming-out experiences given the criticisms of the IGB campaign. There was additionally very little ethno-racial diversity represented, an important factor discussed in more detail in chapter four.

Social media has led to an overabundance of content created and shared online. With this amount of content existing, the algorithms of the sites that house them become essential in determining what content gets viewed and how often it gets viewed. This notion that the archive housing media artifacts contains power over how it is received and how discourses are formed is not a new one. Sekula, for example, found that studying the archive that housed photographs particularly useful in regard to understanding the practices of classifying and selecting photographs for inclusion (Sekula 2009). As he illustrates, despite often viewed and treated as nonpolitical and neutral, the process of selecting and categorizing certain images "exerts a basic influence on the character of the truths and pleasures experienced in looking at photographs, especially today, when photographic books and exhibitions are being assembled from archives at an unprecedented rate" (Sekula 2009, 444). This statement is even more applicable now as all individuals are essentially their own archivists on social media, which in itself adds extra layers to the equation. Through the apparatuses and technologies of these sites, they control the shape of the discourse that plays out, as well as how individuals are able to interact with it (Rose 2012). The logics of each social network ultimately work to shape the discourse that happens. For example, on Facebook, the most recent comments to a post are shown first and one has to go through extra steps to see the original content that fueled the conversation. The conversation that is able to play out is different from one if the comments were shown in chronological order.

One of the most striking observations from these videos was the consistent format they followed: some type of introduction explaining what the individual would be doing (occasionally via text on the screen, but most often by speaking directly to the camera) and some type of concluding remarks from the individual. This always occurred in the same physical location as the actual coming out, and these elements helped to frame and bookend the actual coming-out portion of the video. This works to solidify the notion that coming out is a planned process that needs to be thought out ahead of time, reinforcing one of the findings that Manning (2015) discovered in his examination of personal recollections of coming out. This is partially due to the nature of these videos as they require the setup of some type of recording device, but it also speaks to the importance attributed to this action—that it should be carefully considered and thought out, not something done on the spur of the moment.

Once past the introductions, the actual coming-out process was remarkably similar in the videos. Almost all of them begin with the individual letting their family member know, either on camera or off camera to get them into the location for filming, that they have someone important to talk to them about. What followed was typically a few moments of anxiety on behalf of the individual as they are struggling to figure out how to tell their parent or siblings about their SOGI. This was heightened in importance by asking questions related to how much they loved them or reminding them of when they had previously told them they loved them. This helps to situate this as a very serious event that, since it is happening "live" has the potential to go poorly. In many of the instances the family member, typically a parent, would be concerned that their child had committed some crime or was in serious danger. This nervousness was often present even when the individual coming out knew of their family's acceptance of homosexuality. In the one instance of the woman who came out as lesbian to her grandparents, the preview to the video sets up her nervousness to the audience before she calls them. Once they are overwhelmingly accepting of her, she ends the video by telling the audience that she should have known that they would be accepting due to the fact that one of her family members was gay and that they had always been very active in the LGBT*Q+ rights movement (BriaAndChrissy 2015). A skeptical view of this video would suggest that she had purposively misled the audience to increase the tension; it is also likely, though, that despite knowing her grandparents' history (if she was, in fact, aware of this before she came out), she was still afraid that it would be different for her—a painful fact that individuals are often confronted with that their parents may accept homosexuality in others but not in their own offspring.

There were a few videos that did not contain this element of anxiety, and the individual comes out in a much more jovial manner. However, potentially due to this, these videos give the feeling of being less authentic—perhaps because they do not fit the ascribed norm of the very serious matter of this issue. This perception could also be due to an incongruency between these less-serious stories and my own personal experiences, causing me to feel skeptical as to their authenticity.

Even though there is quite a bit of set up to the videos, the declaration that "I'm gay" or "lesbian" or "transgender" typically appears very early in the videos, with the remainder of the time containing a discussion between the two or more individuals. This discussion almost always consisted of the individual who had come out asking their family member (typically a parent) about their thoughts, desiring to get instant approval. This was a desire that was often gratified; one video was an exception in which the father did not wish to discuss the topic, wishing to have more time to contemplate and assess his feelings (Brooklyn Beauty 2013).

The talking points were very similar in most of the videos, with one of the most common ones was a discussion of whether the family member had already known. What often resulted was the explanation that they had known, but that it was not their place to ask. It should be noted here that this was not the case with the two transgender individuals who came out, and this conversation did not happen in either of those videos. This also seems to support the findings of Manning (2015), in which he discovered that relatively few people were pulled out of the closet, but that it was almost always the individual making the decision to disclose their sexuality, even when family members or friends suspected. This also reinforced the ritualistic notion of the event as it rarely happens spontaneously, but is instead a carefully planned event, regardless of the receiving party's awareness of this secret.

Since there are major similarities between coming out and the religious confessional, it is important to examine the important power dynamic involved in this act that unfortunately Manning does not address when articulating his typology of coming out (Manning 2015). As evidenced in these videos, and drawing upon the work of Manning, it is clear that there is a power differential between the individual coming out and the person for whom they are doing this. We must consider the words of Foucault on the importance of confession, but we must also remember that the subject being confessed is typically considered outside of normal behavior. Here we can see the individual struggling with their SOGI must confess to "abnormality" to their loved ones in hopes of receiving some type of absolution (in the form of acceptance) for this disclosure. There is a tangible power dynamic involved with family member having the ability to offer acceptance and the one confessing feeling compelled to have to do so.

In addition to the format of how one comes out being ritualistic, there additionally seems to be a ritualized dialogue that has developed, especially between parents and their LGBT*Q+ children, that also seems to conscribe a particular type of coming out that has become acceptable. Arguably the most nerve-racking coming-out experience is when one comes out to one's parents, especially for a teenager who lives at home and is financially dependent upon the support of their parents. This is likely why the individuals in the videos that are the most nervous to reveal this part of their identity are the ones who are coming out to their parents. For this reason, I will be focusing on the discourse that has become ritualistic between parents and their LGBT*Q+ children, clearly noting, though, that these discourses were not the same as when coming out to siblings or grandparents.

A major theme that arises from the dialogue between the parents and their children after coming out is how dangerous and bigoted the world is for those within the LGBT*Q+ community. This topic appeared several times in each of the videos that contained a lengthy conversation between the parents and the children. An often-expressed sentiment from the one coming out was the idea that this life was not a chosen one, and if the individual could, he/she would "obviously" choose the path of being straight. The parents also expressed similar concerns and made it clear that they were not disappointed in this revelation, but that it did worry them as the world is not a safe place for LGBT*Q+ individuals, making it a particularly challenging life—a sentiment distinct from that expressed in the IGB videos. Albeit seemingly good intentioned on the behalf of the parents (who do not know that they are being recorded), this statement does serve to reinforce the idea that life is harder for LGBT*Q+ individuals, which, despite the best of intentions from these video producers, could lead to those struggling with their sexuality to feel that life is hopeless—especially if they are legitimately concerned about serious, negative consequences from their parents.

Another commonality between these videos, especially the ones of gay men coming out to a parent, was the assertion that he was a still a virgin. While it could be easy to dismiss this statement as simply a teenager being uncomfortable discussing their sex life with their parents, I do not think it is that simple. This statement serves two main purposes in reasserting both the masculinity of the child as well as their prescription to the main heteronormative, Protestant values embedded within mainstream American cultures: monogamy and chastity. By reasserting their chastity, the men are essentially reassuring their parents that they have not yet been penetrated, an action often viewed as a threat to masculinity. This confirmation of virginity seems to also work to distance themselves from the gay male stereotypes of hypersexualized lifestyles that are at odds with the very heteronormative values of monogamy and family (Halberstam 2005).

Throughout all the videos, there was notable discomfort for all parties involved. Since many parents expressed prior suspicions about SOGI, it was clear they had anxiety about the day that this conversation would finally happen. All the parents who indicated prior knowledge or suspicion also indicated feeling a sense of inappropriateness on their part to broach the topic. Additionally, one of the parents had indicated previous preparation for such a day by watching coming-out videos on YouTube (mallow610 2012). This suggests that not only are these videos important to the individuals who are struggling with how to come out, but rather they also have the potential to become important for informing individuals' reactions.

No videos of an individual coming out as bisexual results from this search. This is interesting to note, especially in light of the criticisms of the IGB campaign highlighting certain kinds of individuals' stories over others, excluding other groups and, therefore, leading them to further feelings of marginality (Wight 2014). As a group that is largely marginalized from both their heterosexual and their homosexual counterparts (Mohr and Rochlen 1999), bisexuals stand to benefit from seeing positive representations. This marginalization of bisexuality is also evident when looking at user comments on the YouTube videos; several individuals posted comments about how it was okay that someone came out as gay or lesbian, but was curious how people would feel if the video had been about a bisexual individual. This indicates a notable dissociation. While homosexuality may have been able to work its way into mainstream society by subscribing to heteronormative values, a concept often referred to as "homonormativity," (Jones 2009; Ng 2013) bisexuality presents a problem—it does not seem to ascribe to those same values since being attracted to both men and women does not seem to equate to living a life of monogamy. In fact, bisexuality is often disregarded as being either nothing more than a stepping-stone to homosexuality or an indication of a sexual addiction (Mohr and Rochlen 1999). Additionally, as many teenagers who are coming out do not necessarily have a firm grasp on their sexual orientation, being able to hear from bisexual individuals would potentially benefit them in exploring their sexuality, as having to "re-come out" as something different is not always the most pleasant experience (McLean 2008).

We live in a society that is obsessed with reality television, celebrities, and social media (Bellah 1996; Couldry 2012). This is especially important as social media contributors, such as those on YouTube, who are starting to take the place of more mainstream celebrities (Ault 2014). This means that there is likely an increasing demand or pressure for individuals to broadcast elements of their lives in hopes of making it big as a YouTube star. The videos that these individuals are posting, by virtue of their location in culture, have the ability to have a much larger impact on the most vulnerable population of the LGBT*Q+ community—the youth who still are financially dependent on their parents.

Another element that becomes very important when examining why these videos are created and the work they do, is to think back to the notion that we are living in a therapy culture that promotes sharing all the personal details about one's life with the world. Despite being about fulfilling some sense of personal happiness or self-acceptance, by sharing these videos, there is also an attempt at building a virtual support group of LGBT*Q+ teens. In some sense it is out of the feelings of generativity that I discussed earlier, but on the other hand, there is also a sense that these individuals who are posting these videos can also find support from the fans of their videos. Even if the reaction from family is not the most positive, there is a virtual safety net to provide acceptance and support. Bellah discusses this need for therapeutic communities:

> The therapeutic conception of community grows out of an old strand of American culture that sees social life as an arrangement for the fulfillment of the needs of individuals. In a "community of interest," self-interested individuals join together to maximize individual good. (Bellah 1996, 134)

In other words, very similar to the goals of the IGB campaign, the goal of these videos is not to fundamentally alter the coming-out experience for the

LGBT*Q+ community, nor is it to promote greater acceptance. Instead, it is to help other individuals gain their own personal happiness by acting as an example and providing a model for how to achieve this happiness.

It is through this forming of communities and seeking (as well as providing) support from other like individuals, that LGBT*Q+ youth are able to safely explore their SOGI (Craig and McInroy 2014). Also, the fact that the individuals in these videos seemed to already be actively engaging with like-minded online communities, either as lurkers or as producers, seems to give credence to the importance of being able to initially explore sexuality without the risk of having to come out face-to-face. However, the fact that these videos are conversations of coming out to family also seems to be an indication that online community is not enough in and of itself, but rather should be seen as a stepping-stone to help individuals as they work toward expressing their gender and sexual identity to others in person.

While these videos do serve to help some teens struggling with their sexual or gender identities, not everyone is equally invited to this therapeutic party. In addition to there being no representations of bisexuality within the videos discovered, the videos were almost entirely made up of seemingly middle-class, white, gay men. That is not to say that more diverse videos do not exist, but, they are not readily available without specifically seeking them out—a task that too often falls on minority populations (Shaw 2015). Since the issues surrounding one's coming out are heavily related to cultural factors such as ethnicity (Grov et al. 2006), having an almost completely homogenous representation when searching videos is problematic.

After watching some of these coming-out videos, Chase, who is not yet out to their family, explained that the ambivalence that these types of videos produced:

> It definitely makes me think, yeah I could definitely come out as well. But it's a little different because of the cultural context. I know a lot of people, like in different geographic locations are watching these kind of coming out stories. And a lot of them are in America or European countries. It gives this kind of imagination that yes, it is acceptable. But they also have to face varying circumstances or even a cruel social reality. It's kind of unfortunate for these people who have to have these kinds of dual experiences. One a moment of empowerment and a moment of devastation after watching those. (personal communication, November 18, 2017)

This devastation that Chase discussed is important because, rather than being powerful and helpful, these videos can serve to remind some of why they cannot come out. Someone who does not fit the mold outlined by the videos might feel that their coming-out experience will be significantly different— or worse, if it does go differently than the videos depict, internalize a rejection as being based on them as a person, rather than rejection based on

ideology. After all, as Bellah (1996) pointed out, we often assume that acceptance or rejection is based on something that is innate about us as a person,
not on ideological beliefs or other circumstances.

While I do not wish to overstate this lack of diversity within the video
sample reviewed for this study, it is telling that the same issues that were
found to be present within IGB (Wight 2014) were similarly found in larger
media representations of the LGBT*Q+ community (Henderson 2013b).
This is consistent with other issues of representation within the LGBT*Q+
community—even when the content is entirely consumer generated.

Beyond lacking racial or ethnic diversity, the lack of variation in the way
individuals come out could also lead to some problems. For example, these
videos seem to promote the sense that in order to gain acceptance for being
homosexual, one also needs to be a virgin. This is problematic for several
reasons, beyond just reinforcing heteronormative values as discussed earlier,
but also to what it means to individuals who are not virgins, or for those who
are still confused about their sexuality. It could lead some individuals to feel
that they need to declare their orientation before they do any experimentation, which could lead to the problem of individuals having to come out again
or having to live in a different closet if they realize that they were wrong
about their sexuality (McLean 2008).

While not explicitly condemning individuals who are in the closet, by
their very nature, videos implicitly reaffirm the hierarchy of gay identities in
which being out is at the top of the pyramid (Cass 1979; Grov et al. 2006).
While I am not suggesting that people stay in the proverbial closet, I do want
to be cautious of messages that preach a need for everyone to come out, as
there are many factors that contribute to how one's coming out will be
received. For some individuals, coming out can have very serious ramifications or be in direct conflict with other key elements of their identity. By
reinforcing this hierarchy, it can force people to come out, when it may in
fact be in the interest of their safety to remain closeted, or it can further
marginalize those not fully out.

NEW SPACES, NEW RISKS

I have largely been focusing on the positive aspects of digital spaces regarding coming out (except for pointing to the often-excluded perspectives of
non-cis, non-white, men). These new spaces do not come without their own
risks and added anxiety. While a virtual space might seem to offer more
security than a public space, such as a bar or a bathhouse, there is an added
dilemma related to online privacy. Many of the most commonly referenced
social media sites used by individuals before coming out publicly were popular, mainstream ones, such as Myspace. This resulted in these individuals

often being concerned about what was public, what was private, and how any post could be interpreted.

When Myspace came out in 2003 as an alternative to Friendster, it took advantage of some of the new technology available and allowed users a customizable experience, including allowances for showcasing favorite songs, top eight friends, and even colors by way of a custom page display (Madrigal 2011). This was under the guise of allowing users to capitalize on their unique personalities and develop a life that they wanted online, in a venue that sought to encompass every aspect of life (Williams 2005). While this was a welcome relief to many, to LGBT*Q+ and questioning youth, it presented another potential front for bullying and the accidental outing of oneself. Since heterosexuality is the proscribed path that everyone is placed upon (Ahmed 2006), deviations from that by children, or even behavior that resonates with stereotypes of LGBT*Q+ individuals, becomes a potential way to out oneself to others. When I was in elementary school, I signed up to take dance lessons at the same studio that my cousins took classes at—on the opposite side of town. Despite not being out at the time (even to myself), I went to great pains to keep this fact hidden from my friends and classmates and remember being mortified when one of my best friends went to the recital (not even on the night that I performed) and saw my picture in the program. I instantly became upset that my parents had placed that "good luck" ad, because it was a new potential threat to increase bullying about my already questionable masculinity—after all I already was not a huge fan of the same action movies many of my other male friends were.

Hiding your SOGI when not out to yourself yet becomes second nature, often under the guise of not wanting to give people reason to question your cis-heterosexuality. Myspace provided individuals the opportunity for a more personalized experience to allow people to feel their interactions were more authentic. The question of authenticity and expression of personality is a tricky question for LGBT*Q+ individuals as there are legitimate reasons to keep aspects of personality hidden, particularly when not out to close friends or family. For this reason, a seemingly innocuous choice of having your favorite songs play, your list of friends be available, and choosing colors to accompany your profile became a potential minefield of self-exposure. Sean explained his fears of what to make available on his social media in high school:

> For the most part I was very very open about everything, except for the gay stuff. So, I would write about my religion at that time, I was open about my struggles in school, kind of . . . you know trying to be good friends with certain people. But I was always. There was always in the back of my mind, knowing that this was public that it could be misconstrued. Especially if there was any kind of gay stuff. That kind of stuff I would write in my personal journal

instead. I knew if there was any inkling of that online . . . back then I was super careful about that. (personal communication, February 20, 2018)

Even though one can take many precautions and use privacy settings to keep their SOGI secret online, there is only so much that one can do and these spaces (and the network logics that operate behind the scenes) can lead, and have led, to accidental outings. Will explained that since they were not out yet to their parents, they had created a second Facebook page unbeknown to family that allowed for posting of gay-related material, such as selfies at gay bars or to have a social space with predominantly gay men. While they were careful to keep these two pages separate from each other, one day they friended a few cousins to whom they were already out. Shortly after, the discreet (i.e., gay) page showed up on their mother's Facebook page as a "suggested friend," resulting in an unexpected outing to their parents—which did not go over well. Sean explained how during the era of Myspace, he also kept a secret and private LiveJournal account during college in which he would write about his sexuality and his new boyfriend. Unfortunately, it was not as private as he had assumed and resulted in an unexpected and confrontational outing to his family.

Under the appearance of protecting kids, software is still working to out kids. As reported by Logo's news outlet, NewNowNext, which reports on issues concerning LGBT*Q+ individuals, Windows 10 included a new feature to allow parents to monitor what their children are doing online. Rather than just blocking certain types of sites or monitoring sites, this feature would send parents an email detailing their children's use of the Internet (Tharrett 2015). As I discussed earlier in this chapter, the Internet and certain social media have become refuges and safe havens for LGBT*Q+ and questioning youth to get information in a safe and private venue. With this new feature, however, if a minor was regularly visiting sites pertaining to LGBT*Q+ issues or contained discussion boards or other forms of social interactions about LGBT*Q+ issues, the parent would receive an email, essentially outing the child before they were ready. This was true even if it was simply curiosity that drove them to these sites.

The coming-out process has long been, and continues to be, an important aspect of LGBT*Q+ culture. It is also one that has continually evolved throughout history with both changing societal attitudes toward LGBT*Q+ individuals and, as I have hoped to have shown in this chapter, with technological changes. Social media has been very influential in the ways and methods people are able to come out; however, the most important contribution is likely the ability for individuals to safely research and connect with others early in the coming-out process to build a social support system. In 2014, a twenty-year-old Daniel Pierce was kicked out of his house and berated for being gay by his family, and this encounter was captured on video and went viral (Ohlheiser 2014). A GoFundMe account was created for him and brought in almost $100,000 to help him afford college. While not unproblematic, it is a perfect example of the ways that social media can, and has, acted as a social safety net for what can often be a scary and crisis-ridden time in a young person's life. However, despite all the good that has come from social media in relation to young people's acceptance of their sexual and gender identities and with their coming out, there also comes new risks of accidental outings. Moreover, there is an added amount of affective labor that comes into play as LGBT*Q+ and questioning individuals are trying to maintain an active life on social media and must question everything they post. It is these added levels of stress that have created noteworthy anxiety about social media for young LGBT*Q+ individuals and caused many of those I interviewed to express their appreciation for and wariness of the way it affected their coming-out experience.

NOTES

1. A "bear" is a gay slang term for a larger, hairier man.

Chapter Four

Let's Get Political

*The Importance of Political Speech in LGBT*Q+ Media*

On March 8, 2018 in the semifinal episode of *RuPaul's Drag Race: All-Stars 3*, California representative Nancy Pelosi visited the queens in the workroom and spoke about the importance of being politically active in addition to the importance of pride and seizing one's own power. She concluded by telling the queens how they are doing just that. This launched a short discussion of the ways in which drag is and has always been a political act. While this was likely an attempt on behalf of Pelosi to pander to the LGBT*Q+ viewers of the show, it also highlighted an important element—the essential nature of political discourse within the LGBT*Q+ community. As I discussed throughout chapter 2, politics has long played an important role within LGBT*Q+-specific media and many of the early periodicals and publications arose out of that political activism (Eaklor 2008; Stewart-Winter 2016). This was expanded throughout the 70s as openly LGBT*Q+ politicians and activists were calling on people to come out for political motivation, an impetus which still exists (Gorkemli 2012; Shilts 2008).

Historically, there has been a division between political media and personal media (e.g., classified ads), but this has been changing with social media's allowance of greater access for individuals to share news and political opinions/leanings (van Dijck 2013). When I initially planned this project, I had not intended to make politics a major component. With the election of President Donald Trump and Vice President Mike Pence in the United States in November 2016, there was a major shift in the political climate for many LGBT*Q+ individuals. Suddenly, the gains that the LGBT*Q+ rights movement had made in previous years under the Obama administration (e.g., repealing the "Defense of Marriage Act" and "Don't Ask, Don't Tell," and the nationwide legalization of same-sex marriage) were catapulted into question as Mike Pence had historically been an antagonist of the LGBT*Q+ community (Drabold 2016). This caused a resurgence of political activism among many of my participants, especially in relation to issues related to LGBT*Q+ issues. Moreover, there had been a series of "bathroom bills" proposed in various states to limit trans* individuals' access to bathrooms in which they would feel safe, racial discrimination and hate crimes within the LGBT*Q+ community, and "religious freedom" bills (one of which was signed into law by then–Indiana governor Mike Pence).

Due to the political challenges facing LGBT*Q+ individuals, combined with the easy access to disseminate information and opinions, it makes sense that social media would become a major source for political discourse. In fact, it was so prevalent that it surfaced in every one of my interviews—even when I was not specifically asking about it. All interviews began as a combination of participant observation and interview. Rather than asking a formal list of questions, I asked the individuals to walk me through their social media usage and engaged in a casual conversation with them about each of the sites as they showed me examples of their interactions. It was during this portion that politics became a hefty topic of discussion, especially regarding Facebook and Twitter usage, but politics became important in every form of social media discussed. In effect, it became clear that the essence of being a queer space made the space inherently and necessarily also a political space.

These political posts fell into several main categories that were comparable to the ones I established within the first chapter, with a small amount of modernization. The two main areas discussed and posted about were either educational or about current political issues. There was also a reappearance of claiming coming out as a political act, particularly in reaction to Trump's election. There was also discussion about nonpolitical posts being political, which I will talk about in more detail at the very end of this chapter.

TIME TO GET EDUCATED

Arguably the most "political" types of post mentioned by my participants were those intended to educate their perceived social media audience. Much as in past LGBT*Q+ periodicals, these educational posts could take many distinct forms and focus on a wide variety of issues pertaining to the entire LGBT*Q+ community. The thing that sets these posts apart from other political posts is that they do not have a direct intention of influencing people's opinions about the subject but rather geared toward educating people about an important element to LGBT*Q+ culture. Many of these posts center around the history of LGBT*Q+ Pride and other important elements of LGBT*Q+ culture, particularly surrounding histories of oppression. There is an oft (mis)quoted and somewhat clichéd saying that, "those who cannot remember the past are condemned to repeat it" (Santayana 1982). The quote is proceeded by a (rather racist)[1] discussion that links progress to historical knowledge. In this discourse, he also mentions that this ability to learn from the past is the domain of adults, where children are not yet able to remember the past and connect it to the present and the elderly are no longer able to remember everything that has happened. It is this generational aspect of his discussion that I would like to focus on, rather than the more racist elements, particularly in how it relates to LGBT*Q+ culture.

A common sentiment expressed was that the younger generation of LGBT*Q+ individuals was losing touch with, or just unknowledgeable about, the past struggles of the community. For this reason, posts about LGBT*Q+ history have become commonplace, particularly among older LGBT*Q+ individuals, to educate the younger generation about the origins of certain rights. Unlike other cultural groups or "families," belonging to the LGBT*Q+ community is not something that happens at birth, and therefore many of the cultural lessons passed between generations are not able to happen in the same way. Despite not being biologically related, those within the LGBT*Q+ community often form their own families with similar functions, particularly with the "older" generations helping to educate the "younger"[2] generations in order to maintain a sense of tradition; according to Ahmed, this transference of knowledge is centered around a politics of grief and grievable loss (Ahmed 2015). For these reasons, the history shared is often not one of creation, but rather one of loss and trauma—AIDS, the Holocaust, the death of Harvey Milk, police abuse, etc.

Without knowing the history of how LGBT*Q+ lives have been lost, overlooked, and violated, it is often feared that the more celebratory aspects of LGBT*Q+ culture (e.g., pride celebrations) will lose their cultural meaning and relevance. These remembrances function as a way of framing, defining, and imagining what the community is around a common sense of historical oppression (Anderson 2016; Butler 2016). It is this communal mourning that works to create a complex emotional history for the LGBT*Q+ community. As Muñoz stated,

Communal mourning, by its very nature, is an immensely complicated text to read, for we do not mourn just one lost object or other, but we also mourn as a "whole"—or, put another way, as a contingent and temporary collection of fragments that is experiencing a loss of its parts. (1999, 73)

It is due to this shared mourning that even individuals who were not alive during the AIDS epidemic or the Holocaust can still feel a sense of loss for the community as a whole, what Derrida would refer to as a politics of memory and inheritance (2006).

EDUCATING OTHERS

While among certain individuals educating about the history of LGBT*Q+ culture was of high importance, many of the people I spoke with placed a high priority on the need to educate friends and family about issues. It was here that they felt social media was an ideal place to reach out and provide information about issues that were affecting them. We live in an age where information is abundant; however, it also means that many individuals are only aware of the information that they want to be aware of or that they seek out (Dean 2005; Gottfied and Shearer 2016; Pew Research Center 2014; Sears and Freedman 1997). Much like online searches are limited by the search terms used, many individuals limit their own awareness by how they choose to seek information. To combat this selective exposure to information, many participants felt that by sharing news that was important to the LGBT*Q+ community, they would be able to increase the awareness in their cisgender, heterosexual friends and families. Sometimes this included layering their own political commentary over current news to contextualize it for their readers; other times the articles were posted simply to provide the information without personal commentary.

When I spoke with people about why they shared these posts or what inspired them to share a news story when they came across it (particularly the less politically involved), the answer was almost always the same: to make people aware of these issues. At the base level, that is exactly what these posts are doing, but they also function at a deeper level, which is to increase visibility of the issues that LGBT*Q+ individuals face in their lives—both domestically and internationally. For a community that already struggles with representation (GLAAD 2017), it is important to be aware that the majority of current representations of LGBT*Q+ individuals within mainstream media are positive (Henderson 2013).

By frequently sharing articles through social media LGBT*Q+ individuals can ensure that these issues will not be forgotten and they can remain visible—a strategy that has always been prominent within the LGBT*Q+ community's political activism. While some shows do deal with legal and social issues related to LGBT*Q+ individuals, Henderson states, "such legal complexities in queer family living are rarely the stuff of broadcast television, even where a season of queer liberalization delivers a majority of openly gay nominees to an Emmy category" (2013, 53). Popular issues are often addressed, such as same-sex marriage (often in a celebratory way) or the desire for gender-affirmation surgery (as has been the plot of several episodes of *Grey's Anatomy*), but these are often on an individual level with the issues resulting from one person objecting to this act. Complex legal and social issues are rarely addressed or even acknowledged within these shows. While *Modern Family* has a gay couple who have adopted a child, the complexities of that adoption are neither addressed nor is there a mention of how there are still many states that limit or prohibit same-sex couples from adopting. Since the majority of LGBT*Q+ representation focuses on middle- to upper-middle class individuals (Henderson 2013), other systemic issues such as access to HIV medication, homelessness, suicide, and the really high levels of violence against trans* people of color are rarely addressed.

The overwhelming presence of these positive portrayals in comparison to the few, niche shows that address the more serious issues can create the notion that the LGBT*Q+ community has achieved equality, with the only issues being a few individuals who are "behind the times."

COMING OUT . . . REVISITED

Since the Prop 8 campaign in the 2008 California election, there has been a sharp return to the politicization of coming out that was called for in the 1970s (Shilts 2008). Several of the individuals I interviewed had only recently come out to their family. While each had their own reasons for not coming out previously, usually due to a fear of rejection or a lack of necessity, the election of Donald Trump and Michael Pence sparked a need to be openly out to their family to take a stand against the perceived potential threat to their rights as LGBT*Q+ citizens.

In her interview, Alicia, who identifies as a white, cisgender, bisexual woman, explained that:

> she went on a date with a woman and a few days after the election was talking to her mom and she came out to her mom as she was describing why she was so upset about the election. She told her mom that she was also into women and sort of beginning a relationship, then moved the conversation on. (field notes from personal communication with Alicia, December 9, 2017)

Hector, who identifies as a Hispanic, cisgender, gay man, also expressed how it was due to the Trump presidential candidacy that he felt the need to make a public declaration of his sexual orientation on Facebook:

> In October of last year, I had a friend, who is a woman, who posted, "Hi. I'm Bisexual." And she was kind of a role model to me. And then I got to thinking, I have to post that I am bisexual or I'm gay [Hector had previously dated women] . . . Am I truly bisexual or am . . . I was thinking and thinking. After Trump won the election . . . that day, that night, everybody was posting across social media. Everyone was shouting concerns. And my friends, most of them are immigrants and come from Latin America. So, there was a real far among them . . . so I said . . . I thought, maybe, if things are going to get worse. I want . . . I need to be fully exposed, so I posted "Hi. I'm gay." And that was

the first time that I posted on my wall where everyone could see. (personal communication, November 13, 2017)

In the 1980s the LGBT*Q+ community coined the phrase, "Silence Equals Death" while fighting for funding to combat the growing AIDS epidemic. This is a strategy that operated under the logic that if the community was loud enough that it could no longer be ignored. Under perceived threats by the Trump/Pence administration, this strategy has surfaced again to make sure that people are aware of the amount of LGBT*Q+ individuals in their lives. It has also expanded to take on a more intersectional approach than solely focusing on LGBT*Q+-specific issues. In a social media post on January 21, 2017, where she came out to more than just close friends and family, Alicia linked her religious beliefs, weight, political ideology, and her bisexuality as all-important parts of her identity that were connected to forms of oppression.

QUEER SPACES ARE POLITICAL SPACES

Social media has become an integral part of our everyday lives, both in how we determine what to do but also with how we share what we are doing. Activities that used to be considered banal are now shared constantly—one only needs to look at Kim Kardashian's Instagram page for countless examples of this (Lofton 2017). Every individual I spoke with throughout my interviews mentioned the use of multiple sites/apps for accessing social media. Moreover, they expressed using social media consistently throughout the day, even to the point of interrupting my interview with them as some received social media messages during our conversation. Each of these sites served very specific purposes. While it has become known, especially in the 2016 presidential election and the following years since, that places such as Facebook and Reddit became hotbeds of political activity, the most striking observation that I noticed was that this line was not as clear as it initially appears.

Apart from one individual, Facebook, Twitter, and Instagram were always the first ones discussed from all of my participants. By the end of each interview, though, each gay or bisexual man also discussed using sites such as Tumblr and "the apps"[3] such as Grindr and Scruff for more "personal" reasons. These sites were often used either for pornography (Tumblr) or for arranging sexual encounters. On the surface, these areas would seem to not be conducive for political exchanges outside of the typical ones you might encounter while acquainting yourself with someone before going on a date. However, these spaces proved to be just as political as many of the other spaces.

"THE APPS" AND PORNOGRAPHY

During the 2016 presidential election, Grindr decided to make their political standpoint known about various issues within the election by live-tweeting of the Vice-Presidential debate. During this venture, Guy Branum, an openly gay comedian, became the voice of Grindr and tweeted, "If Donald Trump gets to deport 16 million people, I want you to think how much hotness would be lost from your @Grindr screen. #VPDebate" (Rodriguez 2016). In other words, white, gay men should be concerned with immigration issues not because of human rights because it might affect their sexual activities. While this tweet is problematic for centering this critique on the white experience (ignoring that of LGBT*Q+ individuals of color), it does showcase how Grindr was attempting to chime into this political discourse.

Fortunately for Grindr, the lesson was learned after the backlash over that tweet, and while they continued to stay involved politically after President Trump's inauguration, the message took on a dissimilar tone. Grindr had been political on its Twitter page almost since its inception. Nonetheless, during the election and during the travel ban that was implemented shortly after Donald Trump took office, this content merged into the app itself, replacing the ads that at one time opened when an individual opened the free version of the app. Shortly after the travel ban was initially enacted, and in response to a rising anti-immigrant sentiment in the country, Grindr featured a short "documentary" series following the experiences of gay immigrants, allowing these individuals to share their stories. This was in an attempt to humanize the immigrant experience for many who would not necessarily be exposed to that element of the story. It also highlights an important issue—while LGBT*Q+ issues have often focused on questions of sexual health, marriage, and bathroom rights, they encompass significantly more than that. Providing an intersectional point of view, Grindr was attempting to demonstrate the many factors of identity that intersect with sexual or gender identities in ways that become complicated and cannot be understood as single identity issues (Cho, Crenshaw, and McCall 2013; Crenshaw 1991; Puar 2012).

Tyler is a porn producer who I interviewed as part of this project who largely used his various social media sites (most notably Tumblr and Twitter) to promote his porn company, Fisting Twinks, which produces specialized porn for individuals interested in fisting. These sites are primarily used to provide free previews of his work to drive business to his paid sites in addition to recruiting potential performers. However, in several instances, Tyler switched up the content he posted on his pornographic Tumblr to make political statements about the history of the LGBT*Q+ community, including the AIDS epidemic (see image 9), pride celebrations, and when Gilbert Baker (the creator of the rainbow flag) died.

My Tumblr page is at times . . . I'll post different things on there. You know. I'm definitely pretty random. I'm a random guy . . . a little disorganized at times. What made me post those things? I think it is just important for people to know our history. I think it is important that millennials know that . . . there is a whole generation that is gone. I just came back from Tulsa, Oklahoma. I was filming a guy there. He is about 56. He was diagnosed with AIDS, or HIV back in '84. And he is still alive. It is a miracle, or whatever you want to call it that he is still alive. He's had HIV for 30-plus years. His face is totally wasted. He's lost all the fat in his face. He looks sick. He looks like he has been doing meth, which he never touches it. And um . . . I wish people . . . I guess the reason I post those things is that we always need to know what happened behind us. You know, that's important . . . to know where we came from because, you know, with this current administration they may set us back 20 or 30 years and we have to keep fighting. Every day we have to fight to have equal rights and equal protection. And, we could lose those things. It's easy to become complacent, because, there are so many people out there who don't like us. I post those things so maybe a few people will just be aware or have an awareness that there are people out there who want to kill us, for lack of a better word. There's people that want to see us dead. (personal communication, December 5, 2017)

Get PrEPped

A major health calamity for the LGBT*Q+ community since the 1980s has been the AIDS crisis, considered now a chronic condition rather than the deadly epidemic it once was. This is largely due to the public intervention by the LGBT*Q+ community in raising awareness and visibility of this once-horrific disease. Despite that it is not as deadly as it was before, it is still an ongoing threat to the health and well-being of all sexually active individuals, with the LGBT*Q+ population disproportionately affected. In 2014, there were over 37,000 new cases of HIV within the United States; 26,000 of those were among gay and bisexual men, of which 10,000 of those were of black gay and bisexual men (HIV.gov 2017). Pre-Exposure Prophylactic (PrEP) drugs for HIV were introduced in 2012 and are used as a preventative measure for individuals who lead a high-risk lifestyle for contracting HIV. PrEP is a once daily pill that can reduce an individual's risk of getting HIV anywhere from 70 percent for intravenous drugs to 90 percent for sexual intercourse (Center for Disease Control 2018). One of the biggest factors in helping to increase sexual health is that PrEP requires an individual to get tested once every three months for all sexually transmitted infections (STIs), which is correlated with significant decreases in new gonorrhea and chlamydia infections, leading scientists to conclude that PrEP is at least partially responsible (Rulli 2017).

Given the health benefits of PrEP and the long tumultuous history the LGBT*Q+ community has with HIV, it only makes sense that this drug would become the center of several social media campaigns. In addition to the organizations that have started social media campaigns such as "Get PrEPped" on Facebook, "the apps" have been active in promoting this drug by enabling individuals to mark on their profile whether or not they are on it. Some also run ads that link to information about the drug and offer resources to find ways to offset the high costs of these drugs. SCRUFF, for example, even featured a video of creator Johnny Scruff discussing the benefits and potential side effects of the drug with a health care professional. Additionally, Grindr has created a feature that will remind users to get tested for HIV and other STIs once every three months. These are just several examples of the ways in which these apps are using the affordances offered to them through their tech platforms not only to allow individuals a connection with others, but also to provide useful and sometimes lifesaving tips and information.

WHAT DOES IT MEAN TO BE POLITICAL?

The LGBT*Q+ community has a long history of political communication and that has only intensified with the proliferation of social media. However, there is much debate over the definition of politics when it comes to social media activism, with claims that there is a disconnect between online discourse and "real-world" results (Samuelson-Cramp and Bolat 2018). Part of this can be attributed to a divide between politicians and the discourses and desires of ordinary citizens (Dean 2005), but it is my contention that it is also due, in large part, to a misconception of what is political. Taking a narrow definition, it is easy to categorize any action that does not result in immediate and tangible political reform as not being political. It would also be easy to examine the cacophony of opinions expressed online and conclude, as Jodi Dean did, that because there is little common terminology, opinions, or priorities, in our hypermediated world there is more division between political beliefs rather than unification or an increase in those who are politically active (2005). Indeed, it is true that political polarization is at an all-time high (Pew Research Center 2014), but it does not necessarily follow that social media has led to a breakdown in political action, particularly among marginalized groups like the LGBT*Q+ community. Instead, it may be necessary to redefine or rather, in the case of the LGBT*Q+ community, to return to a different understanding of politics. Writing in 1969 around the same time as the LGBT*Q+ rights movement launched into the national spotlight, Carol Hanisch popularized the notion that "the personal is political," which worked to shape leftist politics over the next several decades (2000).

Visibility

Initially created among feminist scholars and activists, "the personal is political" is a notion that translated well into the LGBT*Q+ community, with the early days of political activism promoting a very personal approach, namely coming out to family and friends (Chauncey 1994; D'Emilio 1998; Shilts 2008; Stewart-Winter 2016). What made this political was not the support systems that formed or the ability to live a more open and authentic life; it was the notion of visibility that truly was considered to be able to make a political difference.

The importance of visibility been an idea that has resurged and gained more prominence in the era of social media, with a renewed call for visibility in the wake of the Prop 8 campaign from 2008 and the numerous bathroom bills proposed within the past five years. Not only has social media enabled this "come out" call to be spread more widely, it also has enabled individuals to come out in more diverse ways. By doing this, these individuals are adding to the national discussion of the LGBT*Q+ experience. Dean, however, does not believe that communication itself is a valid form of political expression.

> When communication serves as the key category for left politics, whether communication be configured as discussion, spectacle, or publicity, this politics ensures its political failure in advance: doing is reduced to talking, to contributing to the media environment, instead of being conceived in terms of, say, occupying military bases, taking over the government, or abandoning the Democratic Party and doing the steady, persistent organizational work of revitalizing the Greens or Socialists. (Dean 2005)

It is clear to Dean, then, that this focus on communicating one's SOGI is not sufficient to count as political action. Many of the actions that individuals have used to either come out or to express their support as an ally (e.g., adding a rainbow filter to a profile picture or sharing their coming-out story) are often in the realm of what is considered slacktivism, (Dean 2005; 2009; Samuelson-Cramp and Bolat 2018). However, the mere act of being visible, especially in regard to the LGBT*Q+ community, can and should be considered a political act. Even though no policy is likely to have changed simply because of individuals adding a rainbow filter to their profile picture on Facebook, when this happened in 2015 in support of the repeal of DOMA, individuals were able to see how many people were in solidarity with this decision. To Dean this would merely be a communicative act, but for individuals who were questioning whether they should come out for fear of being rejected by their family, this simple communicative action allowed individuals to feel supported and not alone.

Visibility for the LGBT*Q+ community in mainstream media is considerably higher than it has ever been in the past (GLAAD 2017), but the difference between real-world visibility and mediated visibility is drastic. While no census in the United States has ever asked questions about SOGI (other than questions that already presumed heterosexual and cisgender, e.g., choosing between male and female as choices for gender), it had been rumored that in 2020 these questions would finally be included. This gave hope to many in the LGBT*Q+ community that they would finally be counted (O'Hara 2017; Johnson 2017; Visser 2017). Shortly after Trump came into office, these questions were removed (Johnson 2017). In 2018, the census committee decided to include one question about sexual orientation (potentially due to the backlash over the removal of other questions), which is couples can indicate if their significant other is same-sex or opposite-sex (Wang 2018). Clearly a step in the right direction, it is nevertheless still limiting those in the LGBT*Q+ community afforded visibility to those in a relationship while completely ignoring others, such as the trans* community.

Another act to increase visibility was in response to the "bathroom bills" introduced around the country to prevent trans* individuals from using public bathrooms consistent with their gender identity. According to the National Conference of State Legislatures, in 2017 alone there were twenty-seven different bills that had been proposed across the United States to limit access to restrooms for trans* individuals and, between 2013 and 2016, "at least 24 states considered 'bathroom bills,' or legislation that would restrict access to multiuser restrooms, locker rooms, and other sex-segregated facilities on the basis of a definition of sex or gender consistent with sex assigned at birth or 'biological sex'" (2017, sec. 3). In an effort to push back against these bills, and to highlight the hypocrisy behind them, there was a social media campaign built around #WeJustNeedToPee; trans* individuals would take selfies in public restrooms with the hopes of raising awareness to the precarious place many trans* individuals occupy and to demonstrate how trans* people have already been using bathrooms assigned to their identified gender (Kellaway 2015). Even though this movement was criticized for placing too much attention on trans* people who were passing[4] and, thus, unlikely endangered by these bills, it did work to create a visual awareness of this issue and help to denounce the idea of the "unseen trans* threat" by increasing the visibility of everyday trans* individuals.

According to Dean, these acts of visual disruption and solidarity, because of the ease with which people can enact them, cause people to feel politically active despite the limitation of their actual political choices (Dean 2005). What Dean fails to acknowledge is that these actions are not always performed in a vacuum devoid of other political actions.

My analysis of the Pew Research Center's 2013 Survey of LGBT Adults shows that 212 out of 1,170 individuals indicated that they regularly discuss LGBT issues on social media. These individuals who actively engage are also more likely to engage in offline political activities. For instance,

73 percent of those active social media users (ASMU) also endorsed membership in an LGBT*Q+ organization, with 56 percent of those individuals having been a member within the past twelve months ASMU were also much more likely to let a company's stances on LGBT*Q+ issues affect their purchases: 84.4 percent stated that they have actively decided to purchase certain products or services because the company was supportive of LGBT*Q+ rights (Pew Research Center 2013). The same percent of respondents also endorsed having chosen not to purchase a product or service (or having engaged in a boycott) because a company was perceived to be anti-LGBT*Q+ (with 82 percent of these individuals having done so within the past twelve months). 72 percent of ASMU also had indicated that they had attended a rally or march in support of LGBT*Q+ issues and had attended a Pride parade or event. Finally, 67 percent of ASMU indicated that they had donated money to politicians or organizations primarily because of their support of LGBT*Q+ issues (see figure 4.1).

Only 18 percent of individuals who participated in the survey indicated that they were ASMU, and unsurprisingly those who did not consider themselves to actively discuss LGBT*Q+ issues online were also unlikely to be involved offline. While more than 26 million people changed their profile photo to include a rainbow flag in 2015 (Dewey, 2015), because of the relatively small percentage of individuals in the LGBT*Q+ community who consider themselves politically active online, the mere act of liking a post,

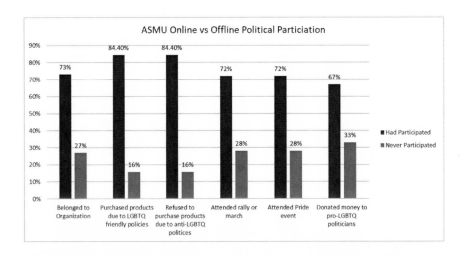

Figure 4.1. Online v. Offline Political Action. Most individuals who claimed to actively post about LGBT*Q+ individuals on social media also had a record of being actively involved in "offline" political activity. Created by Patrick M. Johnson. 2019.

sharing a post, or changing the filter on your profile photo is not likely to be considered by the users as being actively engaged, as Dean implies that it does. What is more likely is that many individuals who are engaging in these activities would otherwise be completely unengaged. Therefore, these acts serve to vastly increase the visibility of communities and issues that would otherwise be difficult to see, and thus easier for the masses to ignore.

Surviving

If we accept that the personal is political and that visibility is a political necessity for the LGBT*Q+ community, another political action that must be considered is one that works to protect and increase the safety of individuals within the community. This is one action that has been very prominent within all forms of social media targeting the LGBT*Q+ community. Given that concerns regarding the health and safety for members within the community have been prominent in LGBT*Q+ media since their beginning, it makes sense that these would continue to be prominent. One of the biggest factors affecting the life expectancy of the LGBT*Q+ population is suicide; LGB youth attempt suicide at rates five times higher than (and consider suicide at rates three times higher than) their heterosexual counterparts (Kann et al. 2016) while 40 percent of trans* individuals report a past suicide attempt (often before the age of twenty-five) (James et al. 2016). Suicide prevention has been at the forefront of LGBT*Q+ social media as evidence by apps like Grindr and SCRUFF advertising for LGBT*Q+-friendly virtual counselors to help those in crisis. Individuals often associate these apps as nothing more than places to exchange nude pictures and find quick, anonymous sex; as demonstrated earlier, though, the political is never far away even in these spaces. In 2017, a story was circulated about a young man on Grindr who began chatting with a man recently diagnosed as HIV-positive and who was currently standing atop the George Washington Bridge ready to jump (Zane 2017). This man proceeded to post this experience on Facebook, which to date has garnered over 1,200 reactions and over ninety comments in response:

> A few nights ago, while relaxing at home, I started messaging a man on Grindr. The conversation started like any other, but then quickly went in a direction that I've never experienced before.
> This man, who is my age, revealed to me that he has recently been diagnosed with HIV and is struggling to accept it. At this point, I started to tell him that I can be an ally if he needs one. But then, he told me that he is messaging me from the George Washington Bridge and that he was planning to jump off and kill himself.
> Immediately, I put on my shoes and jacket, then ran a few blocks to the bridge. I frantically started looking for him in the dark, hoping that he hadn't

already jumped or that I wouldn't be witnessing him jump as I approached him.

I quickly spotted a person wearing a hoodie leaning against the railing. I ran up to him and stopped to look at his face to make sure this was the man I was talking to. When he looked up at me and I saw he had been crying, I knew this was the man I was talking to on the phone.

At that moment, I grabbed him and hugged him for what felt like 5 minutes as he cried on my shoulder. Without any hesitation, I convinced this man to get off the bridge and come back to my apartment to talk with me.

Come to find out, this man is an undocumented immigrant who fled his country after his family ousted him and his brother tried killing him for being a gay man. After listening to his story, I was speechless. There was nothing in my life that is comparable to what this person has experienced, so I struggled to think of any words to say. All I could do was listen. We talked for a few hours, and by the end of it, I assured him that he should never feel lonely again because I will be his friend, and I meant that sincerely.

That night on the George Washington Bridge will stay with me forever and has taught me that we all have times when we feel life is against us. Here was a person who wanted to die, but I helped him live. I may have changed this man's life, but I wonder if he knows that he changed my life too.

Be grateful for your life and everyone in it. Hug your friends and family a little closer. (Blank 2017)

At first glance this post may just read as a person committing a good deed. However, I do not feel it should be reduced to simply a good deed, but rather the result of a culture that has become reinforced through social media, its interactions, and even its advertising. Being on "the apps" means that one needs to be ready to encounter situations like the one that Blank did in 2017 at any given moment. One moment you can be flirting with a few individuals and the next you can receive a suicide warning. I know this from personal experience in addition to numerous anecdotes from friends, as well as public postings such as the one Blank posted.

One night I was chatting on SCRUFF with a friend when I received a message from an unknown person (who was not located in my current city); he indicated that his husband was cheating on him and that he could not get in touch with him. He asked me to tell his husband that he said "goodbye" and that he would be committing suicide that evening. Since he was nearly one thousand miles away, I did not have the same options that Blank did and I did not even know the man with whom he was trying to get in touch, despite living in the same city as he did. After sending him the contact information for the national suicide hotline, I spent the evening trying to track down this man he referenced in hopes he would be able to help this man who messaged me. While I was relieved that this situation did not likely end in a suicide, as I have known too many gay individuals who have ended or attempted to end their lives, it nonetheless highlights the way that this is ever present within LGBT*Q+ culture.

My experience is all too common within the LGBT*Q+ community and highlights the emotional labor often placed upon individuals within the LGBT*Q+ community. The previous chapter discussed individuals making coming-out videos and sharing them on YouTube. A large portion of this was done with the intention of helping others understand that they were not alone or an abomination. A common message that LGBT*Q+ youth individuals receive from politicians in the United States is that the LGBT*Q+ community is ruining our society (Fitzsimons 2019). While rates of mental illness within the LGBT*Q+ community are higher than those of their cis, heterosexual counterparts, it is often claimed by many that the mental illness stems from being LGBT*Q+. This means that to those individuals, the increased rate of suicide within the community is not an issue that society needs to deal with, but rather one that is resulting from the moral failings of the LGBT*Q+ individuals themselves. Outside of the LGBT*Q+ community and its allies, little work is done by outsiders to create political solutions. As such, this epidemic is often left for those within the community who have survived to care for themselves and the rest of the community.

I am not claiming that helping an individual out is necessarily a political action, but the fact that we, as LGBT*Q+ citizens, are primed to be ready to deal with these situations is political. The focus in nontraditional political spaces on suicide and mental health awareness is an act that, if not inherently political, undoubtedly has political ramifications. In addition to these encounters and dealing with suicide and violence prevention in general, the focus on PrEP and other measures for protection from STIs indicates the strong focus among content producers and individual consumers on ensuring the survival of the LGBT*Q+ community.

In 2017, Georgia state representative Betty Price suggested quarantining individuals who had HIV, because "It's almost frightening the number of people who are living that are . . . carriers with the potential to spread . . . whereas in the past, they died more readily, and then at that point, they're not posing a risk" (Armus 2017). Despite later retracting these statements Price is not the only person suggesting that individuals living with HIV, a common dog whistle for the LGBT*Q+ community, should die or be killed. In the summer of 2016, after the Pulse nightclub shooting in which forty-nine individuals, mostly gay, Latino men, were murdered, Pastor Kenneth Adkins declared that the victims got what they deserved (Taylor 2017). In autumn of 2017, President Trump allegedly made an off-the-cuff joke about Vice President Mike Pence wanting to hang all gay people (Brammer 2017). Earlier that year in May, a high school teacher in San Luis Obispo, CA, wrote a letter to the student newspaper for a special edition focused on LGBT*Q+ issues. In it, he quoted a Bible verse stating that gay individuals should die

(Wilson 2017). And in 2017, there were at least twenty-eight trans* individuals who were murdered in the United States, and in the first three months of 2018, at least seven trans* individuals were reported to have been violently killed (Human Rights Campaign 2018).

There are numerous examples of times that individuals have publicly spoken out and called for (or at least suggested) that the LGBT*Q+ population should be put to death. This is not a new trend, and in 2015 Scott Calonico released a short documentary, When *AIDS Was Funny*, which brought to light the callous way the Reagan administration treated AIDS, jokingly denoted as "the gay plague" for years as the deaths from AIDS soared to over four thousand individuals (Lawson 2015). Because of the lack of federal help for LGBT*Q+ issues such as HIV, suicides, or homicides, it fell upon the LGBT*Q+ community to help themselves survive. This was done in part by courting politicians and nonprofit agencies for funding to fight for policies and lifesaving drugs (Stewart-Winter 2016), but it also was done through our media by asking the community to help each other. Survival, thus, should be seen as a political action—particularly for a community whose existence has been threatened repeatedly and continues to fall under attack.

Matthew, who identifies as a black, cisgender, gay male is very active on social media and often uses it to make try to promote a message of positivity that he thinks is important for everyone to be aware of. As part of this he tries to preach a message of survival and overcoming issues that may have affected people's pasts.

> I use Facebook all the time. Originally, I probably used these platforms way better than I currently do. Even though I am still very active, I will often post something and then it will be hours before I pay attention to it again. If I post something political, and then it will blow up and I have to come back hours later and read through that shit and comment on whatever they say or whatever. . . . I would like to think that one of the main things that I do on social media is put out the message that I want to push out which is all about positivity, and acceptance. That's what I really use it for and I really do a good job of that. . . . Pretty much any of my social media is used to show that world that no matter what your background is, you can still . . . you don't have to be a victim of your circumstance. So that would be the main reason why . . . I can stand on a corner and give my testimony and only the people on that corner will hear that testimony. But if I go on social media and I give that testimony, that can reach a whole broader spectrum of people. And despite what my background is, which is very complicated, I still have this amazing ability to love and give love. To love people. And so, I want to push that. I think that love is important. I think it is important that we love ourselves. That we love other people. I can't really push this message of love if I didn't first learn how to love myself. So, that really is why I use it. (personal communication, February 3, 2018)

Dean argues that interacting with others through media only feels like action because it gives us pleasure and tricks us into thinking that we are making a difference (2005). The notion that our digital actions could have a real-world impact is just delusion brought about by our fetishization of technology (Dean, 2005). However, what Dean does not consider is that while these actions might not result in immediate, large scale political change, they do have the potential for small results that can change, or even save, someone's life.

After watching the videos that he credits with saving his life, Cameron decided to go on and create a series of videos to help other individuals in a similar situation. This was also demonstrated in the candid coming-out videos on YouTube that I analyzed, in which many of the individuals only created a video after finding help and solace from other similar videos. While such actions as taking over a military base or organizing for an underrepresented political party are dramatic ways to have a potential large impact on the political world, they still are not able to address the immediate life-threatening pressures for young LGBT*Q+ individuals in the same way that communicative acts can. When the basic needs in Maslow's hierarchy of needs (e.g., food, safety, shelter) have not been met, they need to be addressed before other larger issues can be addressed—and many in the LGBT*Q+ community are still struggling to achieve these base-level necessities. There is a sense of generativity in the way the LGBT*Q+ community uses social media to look out for and protect themselves. For a community that has had its very existence threatened throughout history, to stand together and fight for and ensure its survival is itself a political act.

NOTES

1. The extended quote reads, "Progress, far from consisting in change, depends on retentiveness. When change is absolute there remains no being to improve and no direction is set for possible improvement: and when experience is not retained, as among savages, infancy is perpetual. Those who cannot remember the past are condemned to repeat it" (Santayana 1982). While this quote was used to falsely explain what set Western civilization apart from the more "savage peoples," it is an idea that holds a lot of weight within our current time period and is often referenced when certain events transpire that are related to ones from history. When I initially decided upon using this quote, I was unaware of the racist and colonial origins of the statement, due to the commonplace way that it is used throughout society. However, it is rather apropos to the hierarchy that is often created within the LGBT*Q+ community between those who have come out and fully embraced their SOGI and those who have not done that (or even did that later in life).

2. "Older" and "younger" have been placed in quotation marks because in relationship to the LGBT*Q+ community they are not always a reference to one's biological age, but can also refer to how recently an individual has "come out."

3. Within the gay community, there are numerous apps that are primarily designed for the purposes of both facilitating dating and sexual encounters. These are commonly referred to as "the apps."

4. "Passing" or "stealth" are terms used to describe trans* individuals who visually conform to the gender standards of their gender identity.

Chapter Five

A Safe Space Online?

Discrimination, Persecution, and Self-Policing

In 2014, Facebook enacted a policy that required users to use their legal names. While not forcing everyone to submit verifiable proof of their identity, they ran automated searches that examined for names that were unlikely to be the real names of individuals. One of the largest groups that was hit by these search bots were drag queens and trans* individuals (not to mention Native Americans) (Grinberg 2014; Holpuch 2015; Wilson 2015). Individuals who triggered this search bot to flag their profile had their accounts suspended until they changed their names and/or provided proof that they were using their legal name. This was done in part because of Mark Zuckerberg's personal belief that an individual's online presence should be an open and authentic portrayal representation of their offline life (McFarland 2014). This notion of authenticity is often referenced in terms of how individuals behave online, despite the challenges of accurately defining it. Zuckerberg, in his definition of authenticity, used it in relationship with the term "open," which is relatively low risk for white, heterosexual, cis-men to do. For LGBT*Q+ individuals, especially LGBT*Q+ individuals of color or those in one of the lesser-known/accepted letters within the LGBT*Q+ umbrella, being fully open online is not a choice that comes without risk. There are many aspects of people's lives that some may not want to be public knowledge, which does not necessarily make them inauthentic—but rather tailoring their online persona to the realities of the world in which they live.

Ahmed explains that the world is structured around compulsory heterosexuality (Ahmed 2006). Ahmed is writing about the "real" world, but we can extend this idea to online and digital spaces that also prioritize heterosexuality and cisgender-ness. And, just as in the real world with the creation of heterotopias for LGBT*Q+ individuals (e.g., bars, clubs, saunas, houses, etc.), queer-centric spaces have been created in the digital realm (Bérubé 2003). Though some criticize these spaces for solely functioning as safe spaces (Dean 2009), they work to allow certain individuals who often do not conform with society's norms to freely express themselves and interact with others who share like experiences (Gudelunas 2012). Because of this desire for marginalized communities to bond and connect with others with similar experiences, there are numerous apps and sites that each target small demographics, or subsections, of the LGBT*Q+ community

Despite a seemingly homogeneous "safe" space that is provided by these queer spaces, as Ahmed also illuminates, the world is not only structured around heterosexuality, but also whiteness (Ahmed 2006). While many of these queer-centric sites do provide safe spaces for white, cisgender, "masculine" men, they can also be new places of anxiety, loneliness, and aggression for LGBT*Q+ individuals of color, trans* individuals, those who are perceived as more "feminine," or those who are HIV-positive. More than just erasure from representation in advertisements and other media messages, these individuals are often attacked over social media, sometimes directly, and other times indirectly, within profiles and status updates. Indeed, there are many aspects of social media that have been helpful for the LGBT*Q+ community in terms of increasing visibility, connections, and the spread of information. It has nonetheless also amplified both the divisions within and the external pressures.

WHAT DOES AUTHENTICITY MEAN?

A term that gets used a lot when thinking about online activity is "authenticity" (Leppänen et al. 2015; Lim et al. 2015; McFarland 2014; Reinecke and Trepte 2014). Even though we live in a world that is driven by branding culture, both from corporations and individuals, there is still a desire to see certain aspects of life as authentic (Banet-Weiser 2012). As Banet-Weiser explains,

> Even if we discard as false a simple opposition between the authentic and the inauthentic, we still must recon with the power of authenticity—of the self, of experience, of relationships. It is a symbolic construct that, even in a cynical age, continues to have cultural value in how we understand our moral frameworks and ourselves, and more generally how we make decisions about how to live our lives. (2012, 5)

While here we are asked to discard the dichotomy between authentic and inauthentic, I would contend that for many individuals there is little middle ground in the way they perceive it. It is this false dichotomy between the two that allows judgments of people's media usage as either being authentic or fake, with the former being considered proper use of social media and the other improper.

When Zuckerberg discussed the need for individuals to be authentic online, what became apparent was the lack of a functional definition of what authenticity means for everyone, and especially how that factors into people's lives. In much of the literature on authenticity, the argument is often structured as a person juggles their need/desire to be popular and the desire to conform to the norm of showing their "real self" online (Leppänen et al. 2015; Lim et al. 2015). According to Lim et al., "a potential disparity and tensions between one's authentic self in the real world and one's online presence has been increasingly noted in various feature articles in the media" (2015, 132). In these theorizations of what is the "authentic" individual, there seems to be, at least at the current moment, a consensus that what happens offline is authentic (save for maybe identity thieves or con artists) and what happens online, since it has the ability to be filtered or edited, has the potential for an infiltration of inauthenticity.

Take for example, the criticisms (Hess 2015) over individuals who post selfies with captions like "woke up like this" when they have clearly done their hair and makeup and strategically positioned themselves for the best angle and optimum lighting. They are discussed as being inauthentic and attempting to fool individuals online into thinking they are more attractive than they actually are. This discussion happens as though this behavior only exists online and only due to the technological affordances of photography filters, readily accessible cameras, and digital, social platforms; however, these same behaviors occur in real life. For instance, the first time a person stays over at a new significant other's home, the morning is often started earlier for both individuals who attempt to secretly leave the bed, sneak off to the bathroom to fix their hair, brush their teeth, and potentially retouch makeup before returning to bed to fall asleep in a "cute" position. These are two acts that are objectively similar and for similar goals—to have other individuals think you wake up looking better than you do. However, the former is described as inauthentic while the latter is usually considered a charming personality trait, with the only difference between the two being the presence of a lens and the broadcasting over social media.

The notion that the "real" life is more authentic than the technologically enabled life is problematic and conjures up the aged argument of Gemeinschaft versus Gesellschafts (Tonnies 2017). In recent years, since the advent of "the apps," many gay men have complained about the ways that such apps have ruined the gay bar, which has, as a result, harmed LGBT*Q+ culture. There is a notion that a culture built around online connections is not authentic and that there is something missing about the ways people "used to interact."

Beyond the longing for a "simpler" and "more real" past, the other issue with assuming that the real world is de facto authentic is that it assumes a level of privilege that is not available to many members of the LGBT*Q+ community. The driving rationale behind Facebook's policy to require legal names was that the only reason one would use an alias would be for inauthentic reasons (e.g., scamming or cyberbullying). This policy, enacted under the leadership of two heterosexual, cisgender, white individuals—Mark Zuckerberg and Cheryl Sandberg—failed to account for the numerous reasons why some individuals may not wish to use their legal name online (Grinberg 2014). For LGBT*Q+ individuals, living an identity that is different than their real-world persona has the potential to be incredibly freeing, affirming, and potentially more authentic. Social media allows individuals to experiment with being their authentic self in a safer way than would often be afforded in the "real" world.

While authenticity could be described as living in one's own truth, there are often societal norms and values attached to this notion that prohibit some from actually occupying their truth if that truth does not conform to what is "normal." One of these is the notion of openness—that to be truly authentic, we need to have our lives open to others—although, as Hess illustrates, there is a notion of being too open:

> The too authentic failed selfie includes those instances where the user has included something too personal, such as the selfie taken in the bathroom with embarrassing products present and the night-out-at-the-bars selfie that accidentally features someone vomiting in the background. (2015, 1635)

What is considered "too personal," however, is subject to interpretation. Clear from the examples that Hess provided is that what is too personal is often what is at odds with the protestant sensibilities of "respectable" US citizens. Whereas it is common knowledge that many individuals use sex toys or may drink too much at bars, these are not considered appropriate photos to share with others and are expected to be censored. Omission of these moments from your life is not considered to be inauthentic, but rather it is expected and a lack of censorship is considered an oversharing and overstepping of boundaries.

The takeaway is that one is expected to share based on what makes society comfortable or provides the information that they want to know. For LGBT*Q+ individuals, the questions over what and when to share as well as with whom, are battles that are ongoing (even though most of my participants stated that they do not care what they share). During each of my interviews, I asked the participants what they share online and if they censored or limited what they shared. With one notable exception, most stated that they did not censor what they shared and they expected individuals to deal with the content. Upon further exploration of this topic, however, it became clear that there were numerous factors that limited what was shared, with whom, and when. Certain topics were off-limits for most individuals to share on most mainstream social media sites and what was considered scandalous for Facebook was considered blasé on sites like Tumblr or apps like Growlr.

At the end of every interview, I asked each participant the same question, which was "Do you consider your usage of social media to be authentic?" Realizing the potentially loaded nature of the question, because culturally there is a right answer, it was no surprise that everyone answered with a quick and resounding "yes." However, I allowed the individuals to self-define what it means to be authentic, which can help us work toward a more inclusive and comprehensive notion of how authenticity is defined and the ways that it is lived.

The first notion that should be dismissed is that authenticity requires openness to all aspects of your life. While an LGBT*Q+ youth who chooses to have two Facebook or Instagram pages: one that is "straight and cis" and the other allowing them to explore other aspects of their identity might seem to be inauthentic on the face of it, it might allow them to be more authentic than what being limited to one page might allow them. Banet-Weiser encourages us to not think about authenticity as a dichotomy (2012), yet when issues like this are discussed it is often set up with terms along this polarity (often with the "straight and cis" profile being deemed as inauthentic). While not completely open, the ideas that are expressed within these profiles still belong to and reflect a portion of that individual and should therefore not be demonized. Additionally with many individuals, particularly those from conservative religions and/or who belong to another already-marginalized population, receiving additional complications to coming out (Grov et al. 2006), the ability to create these multiple sites of expression through social media might actually allow them to express all aspects of their personality in the most "authentic" way possible.

Within the LGBT*Q+ community, particularly among white, cisgender, gay men there is criticism over individuals who do not post face pictures on "the apps" as not being their authentic self. While it is not unreasonable to want people to share a face picture with you (I myself require that when talking with individuals) to discriminate against individuals who do not publicly post their face online is the result of privilege. There are many reasons, other than being inauthentic, that one may not wish to have their identity broadcast across social media platforms—even ones that are intended for gay-specific audiences (e.g., not being out, having gotten out of an abusive relationship, or being interested in more less mainstream sexual acts). Posting a face picture online, especially when it can be associated with sensitive and personal information (e.g., HIV status, fetishes, location) involves a relinquishing of power. The information that you have shared is now available for individuals to take and do with what they please. For individuals who are subject to discrimination from both outside and within, this can be problematic as it can open them up to attacks outside of their locus of control. By limiting and controlling what and when information gets shared, these individuals are seeking to be able to stay in control and retain some power over their own representation.

APPROPRIATE MEDIA USAGE

Outside the requirement of a perceivable authenticity, there was also a notion of what constitute an appropriate use of social media. Apart from Tyler, who runs the porn site fistingtwinks.com and used his social media for promotion and recruitment, most individuals who I interviewed glossed over their use of Tumblr to find porn and even the use of "the apps." Even though, by their own definition, these apps and sites meet all the qualifications for social media, these specific uses were often left to the end of the conversation and almost always with additional explanation.

In almost every interview there was an implied sense about proper uses of social media, which was reflected in the image that the participants projected in much of the interview. Many apps and sites are commonly used for sexual encounters or to view pornography, the way the participants spoke of these uses made it clear that these uses were not considered proper or appropriate, but rather were deviant to social mores. When these more "deviant" uses of social media were broached, it was almost always qualified with statements about how that was not the main use of social media or questioning whether that was even of interest to me.

> Currently just on Scruff and Grindr, and just us it for what it is, a hookup app. You know . . . haven't had the proudest moments from being on those sites, but that is what they are there for, I guess. Nobody proudly says that they are on them. (Cameron, personal communication, January 31, 2018)

This downplay of viewing pornography and connecting with others for sexual encounters, both of which were prominent foundations of early gay culture in the United States (Bérubé 2003; Chauncey 1994; D'Emilio 1998; Howard 2001), is likely due to two reasons. The first is the Protestant founding of traditional American values that emphasizes hard work and productivity while demonizing idleness. Even if in their free time individuals are expected to be productive and make the full use of their time (Thompson 1967). Additionally, sexual activity within the United States has also historically been stigmatized as deviant if it occurs outside of procreative reasons (and even for procreation if it happens too frequently) (Barker-Benfield 1972; Briggs 2002; Carter 2007). This puts pornography and casual sex in opposition to two foundational US values. The additional factors of the stereotype of the LGBT*Q+ community (particularly of gay men) being hypersexual and the emphasis on monogamous relationships as a result of the push for same-sex marriage intensify this desire to portray oneself as an upstanding citizen.

These narratives that are crafted by these participants, however, should not be regarded as inauthentic nor as a deliberate attempt to mislead my interpretations. Rather, these crafted narratives are indications of the way that cultural norms affect the way we represent ourselves to each other, both in person and online. Other than Seth Tyler, there were two individuals who were relatively open with me about their viewing of pornography and their use of "the apps," both of whom were close personal friends of mine. This closeness likely allowed for a break from the common and accepted narrative that social media is not used as a waste of time or for prurient reasons.

The second notion of authenticity that needs to be dismissed is that it can or should be judged from the outside. Even though all the participants re-ported being authentic in their online presence, they all also admitted to custom tailoring what was shared, with whom, and when—including those individuals who in the beginning stated that they do not censor themselves online. As Butler reminds us, everyone is performing their identity (Butler 1988) and no once performance will ever be wholly honest and truthful.

THERE'S A SITE FOR THAT

One of the advantages of social media in terms of presenting aspects of one's personality is that there are a vast number of differing sites and apps that individuals use for social networking. In his testimony before congress on April 10, 2018, in light of the Cambridge Analytica data breach, Mark Zuck-erberg stated that the average American uses eight different apps to connect with and stay in touch with people (Zuckerberg 2018). Zuckerberg was speaking about American citizens in general and referencing apps such as Facebook, Instagram, Twitter, and LinkedIn. For the LGBT*Q+ community, there exists a plethora of other, LGBTQ-specific apps that exist to cater to specific niches within the community. These range from Growlr (an app for gay and trans* men who are attracted to "bears"), Trans (a trans* specific dating app), Bristlr (an app for gay and trans* men who like men with beards), and Wing Ma'am (an app for lesbian women) (Mathews 2015).

During his testimony, Zuckerberg and Senator Lindsey Graham debated over whether Facebook had a monopoly on social media—or rather, a monopoly on the types of interactions that Facebook enabled (Zuckerberg 2018). This question went unanswered as it is a concept from the business world that does not translate neatly into the ever-changing, user-driven world of social media. Rarely do any two social media platforms offer the same experience for their users, which often results in individuals using each one in different ways—even apps that seem to offer very similar uses.

At the start of each interview, I began by asking each participant to describe their social media usage and what sites/apps they use. During this time, each person would explain how they use each site, for instance people tended to use Facebook primarily for purposes of staying in touch with friends and family; Twitter was used to engage in political discussions or follow celebrities; Instagram was used for more personal gratifications (such as following cute animals or attractive men); and Tumblr was used to follow artists or for pornography. Even LGBTQ-specific apps were used for different reasons. For example, Grindr was used often for quick hookups, but apps like Growlr were used for making friends, chatting, and while traveling.

Some sites, particularly ones such as Tumblr, were often used for lurking (the act of just viewing, and not creating, content), and others, particularly Facebook, were used to create content with the potential of sparking discussions. Focusing mainly on the ones in which content was created, each site allowed someone to express a different side of themselves and inspired them to change levels of privacy. Facebook was considered one of the most sensitive sites and individuals were generally cautious about what was posted and its potential audience. For instance, on Facebook people would keep their family in a group separate from their friends who were in a group separate from coworkers. This allowed people to decide which of their friends would be able to see what information. There was also a hesitancy in adding people as friends who they did not know personally or at least who did not have numerous mutual friends. Matthew also indicated that he now researches all potential friends if he does not know them personally.

> I feel like with my energy I cannot just let anyone into my life. That is the same thing with social media . . . if it is someone I know and I know I've had an interaction with I will accept them. But if its somebody . . . it depends on how many mutual friends. Because I have found that us talking about gay rights, issues around police and people of color, that I have come to find that there are a lot of people that don't see things the way that I do. Which is fine. That is fine. We can all have difference in opinion. However, so many people in social media their opinions are based in ignorance. So many people don't even do any research. So, because of that aspect, that's when I have to become more careful of who I accept. So now, I'm like we have this mutual friend and I'm looking at their pictures. I'm looking to see if there are things that have anti-gay messages or, not if they are necessarily anti-Black Lives Matter, but just anti people having rights. (personal communication, February 3, 2018)

Instagram, on the other hand, was more likely to be public or have fewer requirements for whom would be allowed to follow them. It was also a space where individuals felt free to post more revealing pictures, either physically or emotionally. Many of the men that I spoke with used Instagram to post shirtless and/or gym selfies, mirroring the types of individuals they often followed, and several of the women and trans* individuals described feeling more open about what could be posted on Instagram from a personal standpoint.

Beth, who identifies as a white, cisgender, lesbian woman, explained how she has felt a pressure to hide her previous heterosexual marriage on some of her social media to avoid the stigma that she is just experimenting with her sexuality.

> Here I am, came out at thirty and mom's like "eww." Still thinks its icky. Weird is her word of choice, like "gay people are so weird." I'm like, well, you know what? I'm fucking gay, so get real. If you think I'm weird, that's fine but then we can't hang out. I think that is a lot of where it comes from. I also think . . . upon meeting new people and be openly gay in Denver and in social circles or whatever. I think that the fact that I have been married to a man before and have been out for so little. It's every lesbian's fear that the woman they are seeing will go back to men . . . like that people will think that I'm not really gay, or whatever . . . Like I don't want people to see my Instagram because I don't want people to know that six months ago I was married to a dude. It's just weird. (personal communication, January 30, 2018)

Beth, who had completely censored her Facebook page of this previous marriage and cleaned out her friends list after her divorce, did not do the same with Instagram. Although she expressed concern over certain people seeing her account and previous photos, she made it clear that it was only women that she was interested in potentially dating that she didn't want to see. She felt on Instagram that she could be completely open and transparent about both her sexual identity and her previous marriage.

Cameron also explained how he shared much of his transformation on Instagram, even though he has been toying with the idea of going stealth in other aspects of his life.

> I think the whole reason I keep myself out and open on Instagram, even though I debate about it all the time, because I can be found, etc. is, visibility is so important for the trans* community I'm in a situation where I feel safe being visible and I honestly would feel a bit guilty if I chose to erase my visibility completely. Because if it wasn't for others being visible before me, I never would have found who I was. (personal communication, January 31, 2018)

Perhaps due to the lack of identifying information on Instagram or its prioritization of photos versus text, it was deemed to be a safer place to share content deemed unsafe on Facebook. Of note, both Instagram and Facebook are owned by the same company.

Facebook did have one common use among almost all participants that I interviewed, which was the use of special interest groups. While not initially cited as a primary use by the participants in their interviews, they all eventually discussed the ways that Facebook enabled queer spaces to exist that allowed them to feel part of a community—either locally or globally. These were all centered around a shared interest ranging from sexual attraction to profession to commerce, providing safe spaces for individuals to interact with others without exposing themselves to the rest of Facebook. In a way, groups like this allowed individuals to feel safe without having to worry about their own privacy settings, because the person who created the group oversaw that. In these spaces people would post revealing selfies, ask for career advice, and even look for places to live and shop. This use of social media harkens back to the early days of LGBT*Q+ periodicals, which often prioritized supporting local, queer businesses and establishments. This works to create a community both online and offline.

THE PRIVILEGE AND TYRANNY OF VISIBILITY

The vast amount of social media that exists as well as the number of active users allow LGBT*Q+ individuals to seek out niche communities and express themselves in free ways that otherwise may have seemed risky. This, however, is not always a positive aspect for many individuals, particularly for those LGBT*Q+ individuals who are also in other marginalized populations, including lower economic classes, race, ethnicity, and those living with HIV.

Despite its common view as a solid identity category, the LGBT*Q+ community is comprised of a diverse group of individuals who span a wide range of other "identity markers," such as race, ethnicity, class, and religion. Often, however, this is overlooked within scholarly research regarding the LGBT*Q+ community, especially in work related to the actions of individuals online. For example, in the edited volume *LGBT Identity and Online New Media*, there is no mention of any of the above-mentioned factors of identity, despite its main focus being on questions of identity in the social media environment that currently exists (Pullen and Cooper 2010). This text is just one of many examples that collapse a diverse group into a falsely stable community, something that has been critiqued by queer scholars of color as not being representative of the experiences of everyone (Ross 2005). To understand the complexities of identity, I turn to two differing theories about identity construction: intersectionalities and assemblages.

Coined by Kimberlé Crenshaw, the term "intersectionality" is an attempt to complicate the notion of single identities (1991). Crenshaw was particularly interested in highlighting the unique positioning of women of color in society, in that they were disadvantaged based on both their gender and race. As many other feminists of color have noted, blanket feminism tends to reflect the experiences of white women and the black rights movement tended to focus on the experiences of black men; black women were being thrust into the background in both situations (Cho, Crenshaw, and McCall 2013; Cohen and Jackson 2015; Crenshaw 1991; Eisenstein 1978). The essential principle of intersectionalities is that all individuals' identities are comprised of various intersections of privileges and oppressions, much like a web of identity. In this way, we can understand that there is rarely an identity that is wholly privileged or wholly oppressed, and thus we cannot take a unidirectional approach to understanding one category of identity, but instead we need to understand that within each category there are many intersecting categories that factor into one's social positioning.

Intersectionality, while an improvement from a one-dimensional understanding of identity, is not without its criticisms. There are two main ones that I will be addressing here: (1) that intersectionality reifies fixed notions of identity and (2) is not able to provide the actual complexities associated with questions of identities (Cho, Crenshaw, and McCall 2013; Nash 2008; Puar 2007, 2012; Robertson and Sgoutas 2012). Some critiques of intersectionality simply label it as a form of "identity politics," in the sense that often intersectionality gets used to locate and advocate for the most disadvantaged group of people while ignoring others. I would like to reject these notions and state that they are merely reflective of the way that this theory has become co-opted by modern neoliberal politics. Instead of dwelling on this critique of a weak version of intersectionality, I instead would like to invoke Jasbir Puar's critique of intersectionalities, in which she not only provides a critique of intersectionality, but provides us with a useful alternative in which to consider identity—the Deleuzian notion of assemblages (2012).

Puar does not suggest, and nor do I, that we should abandon intersectionality, but rather that we can reconceptualize it as something less static and less focused on difference, which ultimately produces more types of subjects, but still requires discrete categories (2012). Returning to Deleuze and Guattari's notion of assemblage, Puar suggests that we need not understand identity as a relationship between fixed identity categories and markers, but rather one that is based on encounters and experiences—after all, if not deciphered through experiences identity categories are without meaning. By highlighting identity categories, intersectionality is fundamentally about the human body, prioritizing that above all else.

> No matter how intersectional our models of subjectivity, no matter how attuned to locational politics of space, place, and scale, these formulations may still limit us if they presume the automatic primacy and singularity of the disciplinary subject and its identitarian interpellation. (Puar 2007, 206)

If we no longer must prioritize the individual subject, new possibilities are opened to understanding identity, especially concerning how that identity extends out beyond our body and into the complex networks of social media. Building upon Ahmed's notion that spaces come to take on the characteristics of those who inhabit them (2006), we begin to see the ways that these social networks begin to embody the characteristics of whiteness and homonormativity.

It is with this in mind that the issue of the ways LGBT*Q+ individuals are represented online become problematic, particularly the focus on cisgender, white, gay men. The It Gets Better Campaign, for example, has been cited as prioritizing white gay men and lesbian women, while obscuring voices of LGB individuals of color and trans* individuals (Puar 2010; Wight 2014). This is an issue that extends beyond this one campaign but permeates much LGBT*Q+ online culture. Much of the criticism over the high visibility of cisgender, white gay and lesbian men and women has focused on the subtle erasure of other identities. As these quotes show, however, there is an additional risk that is related in that this lack of other representations could cause further depression and anxiety.

SPACES OF EXCLUSION

More than just a lack of representation in many channels, many individuals are actively excluded, attacked, or discriminated against within many platforms. In the summer of 2017, a new app for gay men, DaddyBear, focused on helping young gay bears find a sugar daddy and vice versa. While clearly serving a very niche group, which is by its very essence exclusionary, DaddyBear decided to ban anyone who was living with HIV (de Koff 2017). This was done under the prejudicial idea that there are no sugar daddies who are living with HIV and, relatedly, they would not desire to be in a relationship with someone who was HIV+ because,

> No one would like to date people living with HIV unless he is living with it . . . Most gay sugar daddies are not living with HIV, so they don't want to bring home any unwanted souvenirs. However, we support that gay men living with HIV have the right to date with other gays with HIV. But many rich and successful gay sugar daddies do not want to date with gay men living with HIV, which is the reason why we launched this app to meet their needs. (Rodriguez 2017)

This feeds into the stereotypes and prejudices that exist within the LGBT*Q+ community that those with HIV are less healthy than others and that serodiscordant relationships cannot work. While the CEO of DaddyBear referenced the needs and desires of his clientele to justify this decision, he did not explicitly state how he knew this was true.

Most LGBT*Q+ sites do not exclude HIV+ individuals; it does not mean that these are safe spaces for these individuals. Despite using these LGBTQ-specific spaces as safe and accepting heterotopias away from the heteronormative values imbued into more mainstream sites, many of the same flaming behaviors still occur (Christopherson 2007; Moore et al. 2012). Largely due to the anonymity offered to individuals, HIV+ individuals as well as LGBT*Q+ individuals of color report receiving high numbers of inflammatory messages.

> I knew that people were racist, because I was in the military. They were racist. But when I moved to predominately white areas was when I realized these motherfuckers are real racists. But not like KKK racists. These are some of the people who were like, I'll be friends with a black person, but you are not good enough for me to be in a relationship with. I'll have sex with you. . . . You're good enough to be in bed with me, but you are not good enough for me to be vulnerable with and spend the rest of my life with. . . . I have had people who have tried to talk to me who if I said I was not interested or didn't respond fast enough, I've had guys call me n****r, like quite a few times. (Matthew, personal communication February 3, 2018)

No Fats, Femmes, or Asians

Some individuals go out of their way to attack certain groups of LGBT*Q+ individuals. However, much of the discrimination that occurs in these spaces is more insidious, much as Hall describes the differences between overt and inferential racism (2000). This inferential discrimination typically occurs under the guise of "preferences" (Allen 2015; Henry 2018; Trott 2017). While these preferences run the gambit for what people are attracted to, they tend to have a few things in common. Preferences typically are phrased as negatives, indicating what people do not like rather than what they do like (e.g., "not into black guys," "no Asians," or "no femmes."). Even when posted as an indication for what type of person they are attracted to, the posts take on the tone of an imperative and are often very limited in scope (e.g., "only into white guys" or "only masculine guys").

Race, body type, perceived masculinity, and HIV status are main categories that individuals create within their profiles as their preferences. There is considerable debate within the community from individuals defending these statuses and statements as uncontrollable preferences and others stating that these are just forms of discrimination in disguise (Allen 2015; Henry 2018; Trott 2017). This debate is nothing new, as statements like these were included within classifieds from the earliest days of LGBT*Q+ periodicals and undoubtedly existed offline. While not fundamentally different, the expression of these perspectives in social media does change the potential reach of these opinions, creating spaces that do not feel welcoming for certain individuals. This is the result of a variety of factors, including receiving antagonistic messages, viewing discriminatory headings and profile names, and receiving a lack of communication within certain apps or sites.

One of the differences with individuals discriminating in social media versus older forms of media is that there are certain technological affordances that allow these prejudicial practices to go unseen. SCRUFF, an app for gay cis- & trans*-men prides themselves on being an inclusive app that offers a social space for many different people, including different body types, trans* individuals, nonbinary users, and HIV+ individuals (Strudwick 2016). Despite claims of inclusivity, SCRUFF offers a feature that allows users to filter out individuals by race and ethnicity. When questioned about why this was a feature on an app that was focused on inclusivity, founders Johnny Skandros (Johnny Scruff) and Eric Silverstreet indicated that this feature was designed to allow individuals to filter based on their preferences. The two founders, both of whom are white, cisgender men, compared ethnic and racial preferences to any other type of attraction, such as body hair (Strudwick 2016).

By comparing race, ethnicity, and masculinity with other markers of attraction works to hide the way that racism, sexism, and homophobia factor into the ways that these preferences are expressed or formed. Omi and Winant (2015) inform us that the US culture has been built on the back of numerous racial projects (and by intersectional extension gendered and sexual projects), which have informed the ways that we think about, not just identity categories, but every aspect of our life. Skandros and Silverstreet acknowledged that racism and discrimination were very real issues in online interactions in their app (Strudwick 2016), but that it was too complicated to actually deal with, which is due to the obtuse, overlapping, and often invisible ways that these racial projects work to structure society, desires, and wants.

Wanting the Other

> Microaggressions are the brief and commonplace daily verbal, behavioral, and environmental indignities, whether intentional or unintentional, that communicate hostile, derogatory, or negative racial, gender, sexual-orientation, and religious slights and insults to the target person or group. (Sue 2010)

While the overt displays of racism and homophobia within social media were problematic to many individuals, equally problematic were the daily microaggressions that made them feel excluded. There were two ways that these microaggressions were experienced: either having people expect them to educate them or being treated as a fetish object. While never done intentionally to ostracize individuals, and often done with the best of intentions, these interactions often alienate people and make them feel othered. Cameron stated that he was often made to feel othered through "the apps."

> On my Grindr and Scruff, I'm open about it [being trans*]. The reason I am using it for, they are going to find out eventually, so why not just put it out there in the first place. I go back and forth with whether or not putting it on there. Because, you know, I mean. Its [*sic*] good because it clears the air. I don't need to have that conversation and be like you know what, let me disclose this to you. There is no disclosure needed, its [*sic*] already disclosed blatantly on my profile. Yet at the same time, I'm fetishized so I'm seeked [*sic*] out for that reason. Which, depending on my mood, sometimes I'll let myself be fetishized, but normally I don't . . . I'm not about that. . . . Back when I was on my OKCupid Tindr, where I was using it to date, right? Negative encounters being I disclose to them and then either they just like ghost me, ask a million freakin question. I'm not there . . . alright, I like to educate people to an extent. When I'm going on a date with someone, I'm not sitting a bar having a drink with you to educate you. . . . With these hookup apps, with gay men, sure. Tons of inappropriate stuff said to me all the time. You know when people hear you are trans* sometimes you become tokenized, right? "Oh, here is this trans* person that I can ask these million questions in my head that I've been curious about." . . . Messaging me out of the blue asking inappropriate stuff. Usually about my genitalia. (personal communication, January 31, 2018)

Education has been a large part of the LGBT*Q+ political agenda for decades, so in some ways it makes sense that this might be expected of individuals. Despite what might be noble intentions, these interactions result in several forms of exclusion. The first is that it denotes the differences within certain (typically HIV+ or trans*) individuals and makes them feel as though they are visitors in a space that is not necessarily for them. They are allowed entry with qualifications, compared to the unfettered access to which many individuals are entitled. Second, there is an implied sense of disinterest or lack of caring in that individuals are not willing to learn on their own accord.

Fetishizing certain bodies, whether based on race, ethnicity, or gender is nothing new and builds on the long tradition of treating certain people as less than their white, cisgender counterparts. A common acronym in gay-specific apps is "BBC," which stands for "Big Black Cock" and is used both from individuals seeking this or individuals claiming to have this. In early 2018, a twitter debate erupted between several gay porn stars over whether this was an acceptable term to say; Max Konnor, a black porn star, stated that it is never appropriate to use this term:

> Honesty moment:
> I hate when guys refer to my dick as BBC or anything along those lines. You
> don't specify the color of a white dick. . . . I am not a fetish. I am a human
> being. (Konnor, Max. Twitter Post. January 17, 2018, 8:12am. shorturl.at/
> mwS05)

His tweet caused several white, gay porn actors to take offense. Austin Wolf
explained that being fetishized and treated as an object is part of the porn
industry and it is what Konnor signed up for (Street 2018). Throughout this
Twitter discourse, there was disagreement over this term from both within
and outside of the porn community. The salient difference between those
with differing opinions was the race/ethnicity of the individuals—men of
color felt the term to be disrespectful and a turnoff, while white men were
quick to defend this term by noting that these black men should be flattered
by this term, such as Big C's response:

> Uch. I agree with @AWOLFOFFICIAL on this one Bro. Unless its [*sic*] in an
> "insulting fashion then . . . Be Thankful People are Interested and Paying.
> Thats [*sic*] a complement [. . .] And people like Sucking MY Big White Dick.
> When they say that It makes me Hard & I shove it in further. Own it! (Big C.
> Twitter Post. January 17, 2018, 2:42pm. shorturl.at/flvFR)

In his response, Big C stated that he gets turned on when people talk about
his "big white dick" and that Konnor should "own [the term]." In absence of
the historical fetishizing or reduction to object status in the way that people
of color and/or trans* individuals have experience, this is easy for white
individuals to state. As hooks informs us,

> Within commodity culture, ethnicity becomes spice, seasoning that can liven
> up the dull dish that is mainstream white culture. Cultural taboos around
> sexuality and desire are transgressed and made explicit as the media bombards
> folk with a message of difference no longer based on the white supremacist
> assumptions that "blondes have more fun." The "real fun" is to be had by
> bringing to surface all those "nasty' unconscious fantasies and longings about
> contact with the Other embedded in the secret (and not so secret) deep struc-
> ture of white supremacy. (hooks 1992, 21)

In this way the admiration of Big C's white cock is a reminder of and
submission to the power of whiteness, while the references to black men's
penises serve as reminders that they are only acceptable for sexual pleasure
and are nothing more than the obsession that white men have over black
body parts. In discussions of desirable encounters with others, when people
of color are desired it is often only due to their body parts or racist notions of
heightened sexuality (e.g., the long-standing stereotype of the "passionate
Latin lover).

The desire to be educated by or sexually pleasured by these individuals reinforces the idea that they occupy a world that is centered around cis-white supremacy and individuals who do not fit that mold are only desirable insomuch as they are able to provide a service. These contacts re-center whiteness and cisgender-ness; they highlight the ways that others do not belong in the same way—under the guise of inclusion.

Conclusion

The More Things Change, the More They Remain the Same

It is often thought that social media, through changing the way we interact, has fundamentally altered the message. After all, as McLuhan stated, "the medium is the message" (McLuhan 1994), so if the medium changes, the message should also be changed. A common sentiment within the gay community has been that "the apps" have been killing the gay bars and queer culture in general (Norman 2015). When I first conjured up the idea for this study, I had assumed that I would find that coming out and expressions of LGBT*Q+ culture had fundamentally changed. In some ways they have, but in many they have not.

LGBT*Q+ culture is now much more visible than it ever has been, which brings with it both new benefits and challenges. Visibility has always been a struggle for the LGBT*Q+ community and has often been a large goal of the modern LGBT*Q+ rights movement. This has been under the notion that the more visible the community is, the less discrimination they will face both from external sources and from that which has been internalized. When you do not see individuals who resemble you in the larger US culture, your presence in culture is essentially erased. While this is problematic for all marginalized groups, it is especially problematic when the dominant narrative about your identity is one that aligns with deviance, misery, and sin.

Increasing the visibility of the LGBT*Q+ community through social media is beneficial in that it acts as an intervention to the epidemic of suicide among LGBT*Q+ teenagers. As questioning teenagers unsure how to process their feelings about their SOGI, the ability to see and interact with others "like them" has shown to have lifesaving ramifications. Social isolation has been shown to be related to depression, morbidity, and mortality (Teo 2013). Since social media has removed limitations for connections based on geography, LGBT*Q+ communities are able to form remotely and provide resources and support for teenagers and others unsure of how they fit into US society.

It is through being able to reach out to individuals both directly and indirectly (simply by becoming more visible) that social media has arguably made its greatest contribution to LGBT*Q+ culture and politics. This is not fundamentally different from previous political aims of LGBT*Q+ politics, however. It has simply increased access to this ability. When theorizing about communicative technology, it is easy to assume that it is going to fundamentally change the nature of communication either for the better or the worse. Social media, and the Internet in general, historically have been anticipated to both liberate and hinder open communication (Brundidge 2010; Gruzd, Wellman, and Takhteyev 2011; Marwick and boyd 2011; Padva 2008).

Rather than fundamentally changing communication, it is more appropriate to think of the changes in terms of volume. Acoustic and electric guitars are used in very different types of music, and it can be said that the invention and adoption of electric guitars changed the face of rock and roll music. Despite this difference the fundamentals of how a guitar is played are ultimately the same—chords and finger positions have not changed, they tend to have the same basic physical structure, and they are played relatively similarly. If one knows how to play an acoustic guitar they can pick up an electric guitar with ease. The change was a result, not of the function of the guitar itself, but of the volume that was then possible.

Similar to the ways the electric guitar changed music, I contend that the change that social media has brought to expressions of LGBT*Q+ identity is not one of form or function, but rather one of amplification and the changes that accompany the new volume. Through my examination of the archival LGBT*Q+ collections, the themes and types of communication that were prevalent were not fundamentally different from the themes that came to light from my contemporary interviews and research on social media. Since the pre-Stonewall day, expressions of LGBT*Q+ culture have often emphasized personal connections, coming out, the need to survive, and the need to be politically active. These are still the cornerstones of LGBTQ-specific communication present in almost every queer corner within social media spaces. Even in spaces that are designed with a specific purpose (e.g., "the apps"), these foundational messages are present.

While the content and intent of messages have not changed, through social media they are able to be broadcast and directed toward new and wider audiences. Partially due to my recruitment through politically minded spaces (e.g., the University of Colorado Boulder, the Denver Queer Exchange) my participants were predominantly very politically active. Many participants used their social media to broadcast messages about issues related to LGBT*Q+ rights, health, and policy to inform both within and outside the community. Social media has given these individuals a larger platform to preach their messages. Through being able to actively engage in these discourses, there is a hope among many that they will be able to change the terms of the conversation, something C. Wright Mills (1972) stated was a necessity for real political change.

While LGBT*Q+ periodicals such as *The Advocate* have always been politically minded, through broadcasting stories in places such as Facebook, Tumblr, and Grindr, the potential exists to exponentially increase visibility. Instead of only being targeted toward a niche community who are likely already interested, political messages have encroached on what had traditionally been considered nonpolitical spaces. All queer spaces now have the potential to be political and provide everyone with the voice to become a spokesperson for a cause, and the participants I spoke with indicated the importance of this. By sharing posts about the AIDS epidemic on his pornographic Tumblr, Seth Tyler demonstrates the ways that LGBT*Q+ individuals are never fully able to escape politics. In this way, LGBT*Q+ users are actively engaged in a world-building project with hope for a better future (Muñoz 2009).

These amplification-afforded messages come with the benefits of turning social media into a powerful tool for political empowerment and survival. Some contend that this amplification leads to a cacophony of issues being constantly broadcast, resulting in an increase in political and emotional fatigue (Dean 2009). This may be the case on the macro level; nevertheless, these judgements are often based on cis-heteronormative standards of what political action should be—large-scale actions enacted to bring about wide-reaching change. For LGBT*Q+ individuals, however, mere survival should be considered a political act. Despite an overall increase in acceptance for LGBT*Q+ individuals in the decades after Stonewall, many in the United States still view and treat LGBT*Q+ citizens as less than. Suicide, homicide, depression, anxiety, substance abuse, and disease still disproportionately affect LGBT*Q+ individuals compared to the rest of the United States population. Having tools that allow people to help protect others in their own community, as well as broadcast these issues to a larger population to create awareness, are important political tools of survival. Examining the political uses of social media within the LGBT*Q+ community helps to provide a new, more inclusive framework for what constitutes political actions—one of caring, support, and survival.

The amplification of political messages has been helpful to many in the LGBT*Q+ community, but it is not without victims. A driving tenet of the modern LGBT*Q+ rights movement has been the need for individuals to come out. This has resulted in coming-out narratives being prioritized as the quintessential LGBT*Q+ story. Pressure has long existed for individuals to come out to everyone, often at the detriment of religious individuals and people of color (Gertler 2014; Grov et al. 2006; Ross 2005). This pressure has increased with individuals sharing their own coming-out stories and experiences, sometimes even recording them with hidden cameras and broadcasting these videos. Done with the intent of helping individuals still in the closet, a narrative is driven forth that unless one is completely out, they are less developed as an LGBT*Q+ person.

This narrative is based on assumptions of US-centric, gender-conforming whiteness; creating additional anxiety for those whose lives do not follow these norms. Trans* individuals have seen an increase in support since the turn of the century, but it is often prioritized for those who have the money, time, and privilege to be able to (or even desire to) conform to societal standards of gender. When Caitlyn Jenner came out via her *Vanity Fair* cover in 2015, she was praised based on how beautiful she was (Biedenharn 2015). The #WeJustNeedToPee Twitter campaign started by highlighting individuals who clearly passed as their gender identity, ignoring those who would not pass. Masculinity, beauty, and whiteness have long been the staples of LGBT*Q+ standards of acceptance—reinforced through portrayals in advertising, entertainment media, and news coverage. Despite hopes that by providing more individuals with the ability to share their stories, there would be an increase in diverse representations, all stories have been amplified, creating an omnipresent white masculinity that deafens and obscures other narratives.

Within this white and masculine landscape, not only are people of color, women, and trans* individuals obscured almost to the point of invisibility, when they do appear they are often at risk of attack. Mirroring a growing trend of a perceived crisis of white masculinity (O'Sullivan 2017), ethnic minorities are often attacked when they occupy queer spaces, under the pretense of preferences (Allen 2015; Henry 2018; Trott 2017). Women and trans* individuals are often also excluded from what are claimed to be inclusive spaces (Leavell 2018). When not openly attacked, the times people of color and trans* individuals are offered admission to these spaces are often as objects to fetishize. They are there for the pleasure and service of white men, who rarely have any regard for their issues.

Foucault (1969, 1990) informed us that discourse shapes reality. Photographs and visuals are especially powerful in projecting cultural norms and values (Christmann 2008; Hasenmueller 1978; Heywood, Sandywell, & Gardiner 2012; Panofsky 1972; Rose 2012). Despite the overall message not changing drastically, the amplification of these images and discourses enhance the power of this reality-making. Social media does allow for counter-hegemonic readings of these texts (Hall 1980); however, it is also clear that these messages become created either in isolation from the dominant messages or in areas that are openly hostile to them.

As I started this project, I came in with the intent to understand how coming out has changed through the proliferation of coming-out narratives in social media. What I learned was that my initial hypothesis and interests were informed by and reflective of my own biases coming from a place of white masculinity. Through meeting with a diverse group of individuals about their experiences with social media, I realized that coming out was only part of the story—and not even a major part for many people. The idea that once someone is out, disregarding that coming out is a process and not a discrete event, they can live their life completely open and honest to their own truth is one that comes with a lot of assumptions. Social media has helped numerous LGBT*Q+ individuals, including all of those I interviewed. At the same time, there was a lot of ambivalence expressed in their attitudes about social media—particularly by those who do not fit the dominant, white, masculine narrative. It was considered both a tool for emancipation and liberation as well as for repression and hatred. It is with this ambivalence in mind that I offer up a few recommendations on how we can use social media and some things that app and site developers should take into consideration.

SOCIAL MEDIA USAGE

There is a tendency to think of social media as something removed from "real life," by placing a screen in between ourselves and those with whom we interact. Additionally, sometimes we just broadcast to an imagined community without realizing the full audience of a post or profile (Gruzd et al. 2011; Marwick and boyd 2011). Social media allows us to feed our most narcissistic tendencies; however, as an already marginalized community, we need to fight the neoliberal tendencies to view it as a space for individuals. Instead, we need to return to the community-focused intent of the original LGBT*Q+ rights movement and bring that into our modern, digital era. Rather than viewing social media as a tool that will allow us to separate ourselves from our fellow citizens, it can be a tool to unite and support the most marginalized among us. Social media cannot only spread messages farther than ever before, but it also offers the possibility to greater exposure to those different from us.

It is by using social media to force ourselves out of our comfort zone and to learn to emphasize with others that we can truly work to create a more empathetic and engaged community. Thinking of social media as an extension of, rather than a separation from, other aspects of our lives can radically change the way it is used. This is something that some participants I interviewed already do, while others created a strict dichotomy between online and offline lives and personas. There is benefit to both approaches, particularly when it comes to issues of safety. Safe exploration of SOGI is a benefit of social media in that it can provide safe spaces of learning and experimentation not often available in the "real" world. Being there to support individuals, truly supporting and understanding their desires, and respecting people's own journeys are ways that social media can be enhanced to craft these safe spaces.

Authenticity is a concept that is often judged for individuals, and those not living according to societal norms are deemed less authentic than others. These judgements are based on cis-heteronormative white standards that do not work for many. Concepts of authenticity and the type of authenticity that is desired are often considered in the designs of social media sites. These factor into decisions on what names are allowed, what types of pictures are allowed, and even the spaces to which people are given access. Representation within the workforce will not fix issues of access and content alone (Shaw 2015), but it is a good starting place. Outside of some LGBTQ-specific sites, social media is largely designed and operated by cisgender, white men who take certain worldviews as given. The ideas fueled by these worldviews are then imbedded within the networks of social media, with little thought of how they affect less-represented individuals (Wight 2014).

Rethinking notions of authenticity and honesty outside these white, cis-heteronormative ideals can provide alternative ways for representation online. By requiring individuals to choose their SOGI as their Facebook status forces individuals to label themselves publicly before they may be ready to do so. It is an option to leave these statuses blank, but, as my participants indicated, blank statuses are often feared to indicate a deviation from the cis-heterosexual norm. This often requires individuals to fear the risk of accidental outings, either real or implied, by leaving these blank, coming out before they feel ready, or lying about their SOGI. The latter is often the one chosen, which takes an emotional toll on these individuals who feel they must lead a lie online.

There is often a desire embedded within social media to mirror the outside, unmediated world. Choices are offered to allow individuals to express every aspect of their identity. Rather than focusing on mirroring the "real" world, social media can push the world forward by creating an idealistic world not bounded by the conventions and ideals of the past. As Muñoz stated, "queerness is essentially about the rejection of a here and now and an insistence on potentiality for another world" (2009, 1). Therefore, a queer social media project should include a strive toward making the online a more ideal and inclusive location.

THERAPEUTIC CONFESSION (REVISITED)

One of the unintended results from my interviews was the declaration by many of my participants about how much they appreciated my interview and that it served as a form of therapy for them. While I was always quick to tell them that I should be the one thanking them for their important contribution to this research and to the LGBT*Q+ community, upon further reflection I realized I should not have been surprised by this response. My original intention was to examine the coming-out experience for individuals from their perspectives, but these interviews ultimately re-created another coming-out moment for them, only this time encouraging active reflection on thoughts and feelings. Despite knowing what these interviews would focus on (and I was relatively open ahead of time about the questions that would be asked), they still appeared to reflect the emotional roller coaster that surrounds these experiences. There is a thought that once one comes out for the first time that it becomes easier, almost to the point of being trivial. Even some of my participants would discuss how they are out and open with their lives. Regardless of these claims, there was almost always a bit of nervousness in the beginning about discussing their coming out and sexuality with me. This could be attributed solely to the interview setting; however, because these more personal questions did not begin any of the interviews, I would suggest that influence was limited. Rather, I wish to contend another interpretation of this nervousness and then later cathartic release.

Throughout LGBT*Q+ media, coming out has become ritualized to the point that it not only becomes an unfair standard of judgment, but the way it is approached is also the same. There are certain areas of your SOGI that are appropriate to reveal to others, and those that are to be remain hidden. Once we enact this ritual, it does become easier (for most) because we have practiced the approved script of being LGBT*Q+ in America. This factors into not only our face-to-face interactions with individuals, but how we portray ourselves online. Expressions of SOGI online, therefore, are also limited by these scripts. What Ahmed referred to as compulsory heterosexuality (2006) and Duggan described as the new homonormativity (2002) have shifted and blended to take on new meaning within the LGBT*Q+ community online: compulsory homonormativity. While it is considered more acceptable to express SOGI, it is only acceptable when done in certain contexts. The importance of this visibility cannot be understated; it is important to remember what remains hidden, however. My interviews allowed many of the feelings, emotions, hopes, and fears surrounding the LGBT*Q+ community to be expressed, resulting in a cathartic release, even if only fleeting.

Smartphones provide nearly constant access to communication platforms, connecting us with people all over the world instantaneously and continuously. This has allowed the spread of ideas and opinions to flourish and has encouraged people to seek others out and form new bonds that otherwise would have been unavailable to them in the past. As was indicated by some of the people I interviewed, this has been a literal lifesaver for some individuals. The LGBT*Q+ community, due to a wider social castigation, is at a heightened risk for anxiety, depression, and other mental disorders. Being able to connect with others who can act as living proof that there is a kinder, more accepting world outside of what may be your own limited geographic sphere can help to reframe one's place in the world. Since the beginning of printed forms of communication, LGBT*Q+ individuals have been using it to connect with LGBT*Q+ individuals. The desire to do this is no different than it has been in the past, but social media and smartphones allow this to happen with people all over the world, providing an oft-needed beacon of hope for some of the more marginalized members of the LGBT*Q+ community.

More than just being used to connect individuals, LGBT*Q+ communication has also pushed forth a narrative of how to be a proper, respectable, and desirable LGBT*Q+ citizen. This has always centered cisgender, middle- to upper-class white men. While white desirability has always been present within most of these discourses, these messages have been amplified by the interconnectedness enabled by social media. Visibility has helped some cope with the social stigma cast upon the LGBT*Q+ community by the larger society, but in a social media-driven world that pretends to make everything connected and visible, some in the community have been cast further aside. Within LGBT*Q+ publications and social media groups, when a topic diverges from the expected cisgender homonormative (and white) path, it is often met with backlash and cries for exclusion. This is often done under the guise of "not helping our community." The identity that has emerged as the dominant figure representing the LGBT*Q+ community is the white, middle-class, gay and/or lesbian couple. When other issues such as immigration rights for LGBT*Q+ individuals, trans* rights, polyamory, fetish communities, and individuals of color are brought to light, they are often faced with statements belittling them or distancing them from the LGBT*Q+ community. When these issues are highlighted, they are often done with the intent of tokenizing or fetishizing them, often by well-intentioned, liberal individuals. These individuals have often had to find specific and niche locations to form their own communities. They are allowed into the mainstream LGBT*Q+ communities, but only if their presence does not threaten the hegemonic, cisgender, white homonormativity present within.

Social media has given voice to millions of LGBT*Q+ Americans and shown a vulnerable and at-risk population that they are not alone and there is hope. It has also created a new script that must be followed in order to gain this acceptance. Deviations from this narrative are confined to less popular apps and the LGBT*Q+-specific apps (the online version of the gay ghetto).

These other aspects of LGBT*Q+ identities are thus relegated, confined, and contained within a new, digital closet.

Afterword

A "Kindr" Online Environment?

In the months following the conclusion of all of my interviews, Grindr, in a response to the criticism of discrimination on their app, launched their Kindr initiative. The purported intent of this was to help shine a light on some of the more vile and negative aspects that were occurring in the app. This covered topics such as racism, transphobia, femme shaming, and body shaming. One of the most direct ways this was tackled was through a short-lived video series on their YouTube channel of users discussing their opinions and experiences with these different topics. There were six episodes in total produced within just over a one-month period (from September 18, 2018 to October 28, 2018). This was done seemingly with two overt intentions. The first was to provide a voice for people who had felt marginalized in the online environment. While this was directed toward Grindr users, based on my interviews and personal interactions online, these stories are not unique to Grindr, but permeate much of LGBT*Q+ social media. There was a direct attempt to not just share the voices from the videos (shot professionally on a soundstage), but to allow everyone to contribute to the conversation by attempting to create a hashtag to coalesce a conversation. #KindrGrindr failed to take off, with only videos produced by Grindr using this on YouTube and just over one hundred images on Instagram in a one-year period from its September 2018 birth.

The hashtag gained a different life on Twitter—likely to the chagrin of Grindr. There was a conversation for a few days where users were discussing their experiences with the platform and encounters with others. However, people were also very quick to point out that this seemed like a publicity stunt for Grindr, given their history of enabling much of this behavior, with some calling it faux activism. For their part, Grindr allegedly hired employees to tackle this issue and, according to their tweets, started engaging with activists to decide how to move forward (hispanic pixie dream girl. Twitter Post. September 18, 2018, 1:23PM. shorturl.at/jlW57). A question that was raised in hispanic pixie dream girl's (Matthew Rodriguez, the employee hired by Grindr to tackle this campaign) was whether Grindr would still provide a filter to exclude or include people based solely on their ethnicity. Rodriguez pointed out that he was aware that this was problematic and mentioned that there were other types of filters that were also problematic (such as body type) and they were working to figure out the future of Grindr's filters. As of August 2019, these filters still remain a feature of the pro version of Grindr (Grindr XTRA).

The second likely intention of this campaign was to educate users (and others) of the issues faced by many individuals online, particularly trans* individuals and POC. By highlighting these issues, Grindr was trying to curb many of these negative behaviors by informing people about the ramifications of phrases such as "No Fats, No Fems, No Asians" or "Not into black guys." Where this effort stopped short was in focusing solely on the expression of these "preferences" without focusing on why there were problematic in the first place. While there were offhand comments about how excluding all Asian people (for example) are problematic because not all Asian individuals look the same, it was also clear that the real issue (according to Grindr) was the statement of these preferences in profiles and conversations—not that individuals had these racist views to begin with.

Despite the lack of removing filters based on ethnicity or body type, Grindr did make a lot of other changes to their app, most notably in their profile section. Now there are numerous options for gender including cis and trans* options for both men and women (including just an unmodified man or woman option) as well as four nonbinary options. Each of the three categories (man, woman, nonbinary) also allow for the creation of a custom label. At the top of the page, there is a link that provides information for those who are unfamiliar with the terminology. This link takes the user to Grindr's help center section on gender identity, which contains articles about all of the different terms. Under the definitions, there are other links for questions including an information about resources for trans* safety and an FAQ section for individuals who are not familiar with trans* issues. Additionally, under the gender drop-down menu for gender identity there is a section for pronouns with the options of "He/Him/His," "She/Her/Hers," "They/Them/Theirs," and the ability for a custom response.

Other options in the profile section allow for individuals to indicate where they would like to meet (including options such as a coffee shop) and whether a user wants to receive explicit (NSFW) images. Additionally, they have retained the ability to indicate your HIV-status and to include a reminder of when you need to be tested again. Much like the gender identity section, this category also provides a link to their help center, which acts as a sexual health resource. This area acts as an educational tool to inform the community and users about various safer-sex resources including questions about consent and a tool to locate an HIV testing center near you (regardless of where in the world you live).

The reporting function of the app also attempts to curb some of the more offensive behaviors, with options to report individuals for harassment/bullying or for hate speech/discrimination. When you click on either option, it provides an explanation of what each category entails and what is not allowed including "discriminatory or bigoted statements." This then allows the user to explain, in their own words, the offensive behavior or statements they encountered. While this seems to clearly pertain to issues of negative discrimination, it is yet to be seen how this will deal with issues of fetishization.

Grindr's Kindr initiative is not perfect by any means, but it does show a desire to move in the direction of acceptance and the creation of a more welcoming social media environment. They are not the only company doing this, but they are also not reflective of the entirety of the LGBT*Q+ social media climate. While some users have taken it upon themselves to use the custom options now provided in the profile section to mock the concept, others have embraced it. While this has not stopped people posting that they are not into certain "types" of people (even if they are now forced to find different ways of stating these "preferences"), it has started to put this terminology into everyday awareness.

BEING AN AWARE SOCIAL MEDIA USER

When I finished this project, I was initially very nervous about how all of the people I worked with would respond to my interpretations. After all, they were opening up about very personal aspects of their lives to me and then allowing me to write about them. One of the things that came out of all the interviews when I was talking with the participants later was that they all really enjoyed the interview and it helped make them more aware of how they were engaging with this technology that is so often a mindless task. In writing this and in talking with everyone, I too have found myself being more self-reflective about what I put online and how I do so. Too often when we are engaging online, we get blinded or distracted by the screen in front of us, and it can be hard to remember that there are other people on the other sides of their own screens who are engaging with us—even if we are not directly talking with them.

While I strongly believe technology companies need to take steps to make social media a more inclusive and welcoming location, it is also our responsibility to help ensure that this happens. Through my time working on this project and talking to so many different people, I realized that my social media habits were changing as well. This got me thinking about some of the best practices that I have picked up along the way and the things I now take into consideration when going online. I have created a list of five different things that we can each do when engaging with diverse groups of individuals both directly and indirectly through social media: We should be Authentic, Well-Intentioned, Accepting, show Restraint, and engage in Earnest communication, or AWARE.

Authentic

I spent quite a bit of time discussing the question of authenticity earlier in this text and I spoke with every single participant about this concept. It is a term that has different meanings for everyone and it can be a confusing and sometimes dangerous method by which to judge other people. I do, however, think it is a useful term when thinking about it on the personal level in regard to what we want to post. Every person I spoke with had their own interpretation of what it meant to be authentic, but most people seemed to think that what they posted was an authentic representation of themselves. I think that this is a great quality to have when deciding what to share, who to engage with, and what to write in our profiles. We should strive to have the online version(s) of ourselves match the offline versions in some way. This is not to say that there has to be just one version of us, but rather I do believe that multiple authentic selves can exist within the same person. What is important is that we are comfortable sharing what we share where we share it.

It is okay to share some things in some places and not others. We do it all the time in our offline lives, so why should online be different? What I think is most important is that we, as users and online citizens, should decide what it means to us to be authentic and not use that same rubric to judge others. We should decide what our truth is and live in and own that truth. For some, that might be creating alternate personas online to express things we otherwise might not due to fear or other anxieties. Social media can provide a great place to explore our identity and play around with it, and we should feel comfortable doing that if we desire to.

Well-Intentioned

There is a saying that the road to hell is paved with good intentions. There is some truth to this, but that does not mean we should not try to act with good intentions. A lot of the negativity that comes out online often results from malice or a lack of foresight. I think it is important to consider that everything we put out online has reactions to it that we cannot control. With the speed of the communication now, if we put something online, within seconds it can spread beyond our control. While this is not always controllable, it should be something that is considered during and before all interactions with others.

The key word in well-intentioned is intention, which means to have a purpose. If we really think about what this means, it means more than just not wanting to hurt others by what we post. It means that every engagement we have online should have some type of purpose. It should be thought about and considered. Before posting a possibly offensive "preference," it is important to consider why you are doing that and the possible outcomes. Similarly, before barraging a trans* individual with questions about their genitals or making sexualized jokes with an someone who is asexual, it is important to stop and consider what the purpose of this conversation is. If the only purpose it serves is for your benefit, perhaps it is something that should not be done.

Accepting

This is a big one. As a cisgender, white male I cannot (nor should I try to) speak for everyone's experiences. It also means that my own experiences are not reflective of the environment that everyone else lives in or that my worldview is reflective of their worldviews. This is important because it means we do not always get to say what is important to others. There is a lot of talk, almost always coming from places of privilege, that there are "more important things to worry about" when small, almost meaningless changes occur (e.g., when people started using the term cisgender or when Berkeley, California, decided to change the term "manhole" to "maintenance hole"). The problem with this way of thinking is that just because something is not important to you does not mean it is not important to other people. We need to be accepting of people's lived experiences and trust them on what they feel is important.

I do not mean, by arguing for acceptance, that we should be accepting of all behavior online. It is why this is not the only guideline I am offering. We need to accept the different lived experiences of people and then ask ourselves the question "how does this affect me?" If this answer is it does not, then we should accept it. If it does negatively affect you, then it should not be simply accepted, but rather something that should be interrogated. A lot of this type of accepting is to place yourself in someone else's position and try to understand where they are coming from with their interactions.

Restraint

Going together with acceptance and being well-intentioned is the idea of showing restraint. Social media is too often viewed by individuals as an individual experience that is designed for individual thoughts to be expressed. I would argue that this is not the case, but rather it is a social or community experience in which we are all experiencing and expressing things with, to, and through each other. For these reasons, it is important to show some restraint in what we express. Before we make a post or send a DM, taking a moment to consider how it will be perceived by others and how it will affect others is important. Too often, social media can become a space to channel our every thought, feeling, picture, or jokes. These are often defended by just one individual expressing what they want to express. This is a right that is protected by the First Amendment (with limitations), but just because something is legal does not mean we should have carte blanche to do so. Words and images have meanings, and we should always consider what those meanings will do once they are out in the real world. It is more than just not sharing things, however. If we think about sharing something or saying something online, and then we stop and restrain ourselves from sharing that because of how others will (or could) perceive it, it is then our responsibility to interrogate that and question what about our experiences made us want to state that in the first place. For example, it seems like some people are starting to understand the problem of stating things like "Not into black guys" or "only like real men." It is good that they are now censoring themselves from saying that, but it is only a small step toward the actual solution, which is for those individuals to take a deep, hard look at why they have those "preferences" in the first place.

Earnest

The final guideline that I will offer in this chapter is that I believe we should be earnest in all our communications. In this I mean that we should take every interaction seriously and we should act according to our convictions. This does not mean that we have to be serious in every interaction, but we should take our actions seriously. Even if we are joking or sharing a meme, it is important to remember that anything that goes out online ultimately becomes a reflection of who we are. The things that we read and engage with, as well as the ways that we do these things, also affect who we are as a person and how we see the world.

This is the biggest lesson that I have taken away from my work on this project, and I have seen my relationship with social media change dramatically. Being a more conscious poster and engaging with sincerity has altered the way that I engage with others and the way that I view myself in social media. This may seem similar to others that I have listed, but I think this one speaks to the values that we hold close to us. Those core values that have shaped our worldviews. If we engage with social media in accordance with those values and understand that what we put out in the social media world has real and sometimes serious consequences, we can begin to enact the changes that everyone I spoke with wants to see online and create more welcoming, inclusive, and safe spaces.

FINAL THOUGHTS

Over the past several decades, both media and cultural norms have changed a lot in some ways and in other ways they have not. I think too often there is a reliance on technology to solve our problems, or it is used as a scapegoat for our problems. The most shocking thing I discovered when doing this research is that despite all of the technological and cultural changes that have occurred since the late 1960s in the United States, people still struggle with the same issues—even if they are different iterations of them. When I saw an ad in *The Advocate* from the 1990s that would have been a relevant and timely meme on Facebook today, I realized that technology is neither the cause nor the solution to problems in society, but merely helps them manifest in different ways.

Every person I spoke with, in some way or other, spoke about the positives and negatives of social media. But the pros or cons were never with the technology themselves. They were always with the people or groups of people on the other sides of their screens many miles away. While it can be easy to blame a new technology for some social change, doing so does not address the root of the problem. There is evidence to show that as social media has developed so too has political polarization increased. But I think we would be foolish to think that social media has caused this polarization. It may contribute to it, but only in that it allows people to interact in new ways. It is also quite possible that we are just becoming more aware of things as we become more connected.

If we truly want social media to be a better place, to live up to the ideals that were believed when it was created, then the changes need to come not just from developers but also from ourselves. Only we are responsible for the content we share, and it is, in my opinion, our responsibility to realize that we cannot view our social media interactions as existing solely for ourselves as individuals, but that they exist as part of this other world that is both attached to and detached from our own lives. Tweets, memes, hashtags, profiles, and pictures all have meanings and lives beyond our intent and our control. It is because of this that I think that if we are to engage in social media, we need to be AWARE about all of the implications of every thing we share.

Bibliography

Ahmed, S. (2006). *Queer phenomenology: Orientations, objects, others.* Duke University Press.

———. (2015). *The cultural politics of emotion* (Second edition). Routledge.

Allen, S. (2015, September 9). 'No Blacks' Is Not a Sexual Preference. It's Racism. *The Daily Beast.* https://www.thedailybeast.com/articles/2015/09/09/no-blacks-is-not-a-sexual-preference-it-s-racism.

And They Call That Gay Pride? (2001, July 6). *Afro-American Red Star*, A14.

Anderson, B. R. O. (2016). *Imagined communities: Reflections on the origin and spread of nationalism* (2 edition). Verso.

Armus, T. (2017, October 21). A Georgia lawmaker responds to backlash over her "quarantine" HIV comment. *NBC News.* https://www.nbcnews.com/feature/nbc-out/georgia-state-rep-betty-price-uses-term-quarantine-asking-about-n812831.

Asala, A. (2010, December 1). LGBT Youth Suicides and Diversity. *Color Magazine.* http://www.colormagazineusa.com/index.php?option=com_content&view=article&id=467.

Attenborough, R. (1985). *A Chorus Line* [Musical]. Columbia Pictures.

Auerbach, D., and Prescott, S. (2014, August 21). When AOL Was GayOL. *Slate.* http://www.slate.com/articles/technology/bitwise/2014/08/lgbtq_nerds_and_the_evolution_of_life_online.html.

Ault, S. (2014, August 5). Survey: YouTube stars more popular than mainstream celebs among U.S. teens. *Variety.* http://variety.com/2014/digital/news/survey-youtube-stars-more-popular-than-mainstream-celebs-among-u-s-teens-1201275245/.

Ball, C. A. (2015). *Obscenity, Morality, and the First Amendment: The First LGBT Rights Cases Before the Supreme Court.* https://papers.ssrn.com/abstract=2591907.

Banet-Weiser, S. (2012). *Authentic TM: Politics and ambivalence in a brand culture.* New York University Press.

Barker-Benfield, B. (1972). The Spermatic Economy: A Nineteenth Century View of Sexuality. *Feminist Studies 1*(1), 45. https://doi.org/10.2307/3180106.

Battles, K., and Hilton-Morrow, W. (2002). Gay Characters in Conventional Spaces: *Will and Grace* and the Situation Comedy Genre. *Critical Studies in Media Communication 19*(1), 87.

Baym, N. K., and boyd, danah. (2012). Socially Mediated Publicness: An Introduction. *Journal of Broadcasting & Electronic Media 56*(3), 320–329. https://doi.org/10.1080/08838151.2012.705200.

Becker, A. B., and Scheufele, D. A. (2009). Moral Politicking: Public Attitudes toward Gay Marriage in an Election Context. *The International Journal of Press/Politics 14*(2), 186–211. https://doi.org/10.1177/1940161208330905.

Becker, R. (2006). *Gay TV and straight America*. Rutgers University Press.

Bellah, R. N. (Ed.). (1996). *Habits of the heart: Individualism and commitment in American life: updated edition with a new introduction* (1st Calif. pbk. ed). University of California Press.

Bérubé, A. (2003). The History of Gay Bathhouses. *Journal of Homosexuality 44*(3–4), 33–53. https://doi.org/10.1300/J082v44n03_03.

Biedenharn, I. (2015, June 3). Jon Stewart slams Caitlyn Jenner media coverage for focusing on her looks. *Entertainment Weekly*. http://www.ew.com/article/2015/06/03/jon-stewart-slams-caitlyn-jenner-media-coverage-focusing-her-looks.

Bird, S. E. (2003). *Audience in everyday life: Living in a media world*. Routledge.

Blank, L. (2017, September 11). *A few nights ago, while relaxing at home, I started messaging a man on Grindr. The conversation started like any other, but then quickly went in a direction that I've never experienced before* [Facebook]. https://www.facebook.com/Liam.Blank/posts/10214902735748251.

Bonds-Raacke, J. M., Cady, E. T., Schlegel, R., Harris, R. J., and Firebaugh, L. (2007). Remembering Gay/Lesbian Media Characters: Can Ellen and Will Improve Attitudes Toward Homosexuals? *Journal of Homosexuality 53*(3), 19–34. https://doi.org/10.1300/J082v53n03_03.

Bonner-Thompson, C. (2017). "The meat market": Production and regulation of masculinities on the Grindr grid in Newcastle-upon-Tyne, UK. *Gender, Place & Culture 24*(11), 1611–1625. https://doi.org/10.1080/0966369X.2017.1356270.

Boyd, D. (2012). The politics of "real names." *Communications of the ACM 55*(8), 29. https://doi.org/10.1145/2240236.2240247.

Brammer, J. P. (2017, October 17). Trump reportedly joked about VP Mike Pence wanting to "hang" gays. *NBC News*. https://www.nbcnews.com/feature/nbc-out/trump-reportedly-jokes-about-mike-pence-wanting-hang-gays-n811086.

Branson-Potts, H. (2015, April 27). "Bruce Jenner did us proud," transgender advocate cheers. *LA Times*. http://www.latimes.com/local/lanow/la-me-ln-bruce-jenner-transgender-community-cheers-20150427-story.html.

BriaAndChrissy. (2015, July 19). *LIVE coming out to my grandma!* https://www.youtube.com/watch?v=XC7W5vUaIxc.

Briggs, L. (2002). *Reproducing empire: Race, sex, science, and U.S. imperialism in Puerto Rico*. University of California Press.

Brooklyn Beauty. (2013, May 14). *Coming out to my dad on camera!* https://www.youtube.com/watch?v=ejAysC7D8sI.

Brundidge, J. (2010). Encountering "Difference" in the Contemporary Public Sphere: The Contribution of the Internet to the Heterogeneity of Political Discussion Networks. *Journal of Communication 60*(4), 680–700. https://doi.org/10.1111/j.1460–2466.2010.01509.x.

Butler, J. (1988). Performative Acts and Gender Constitution: An Essay in Phenomenology and Feminist Theory. *Theater Journal 40*(4), 519–531.

———. (2016). *Frames of war: When is life grievable?* Verso.

Carosone, M. (2013, September 25). Yes, Suicide Is a Gay Issue. *Huffington Post*. http://www.huffingtonpost.com/michael-carosone/yes-suicide-is-a-gay-issue_b_3975312.html.

Carter, J. (2007). *The heart of whiteness: Normal sexuality and race in America, 1880–1940*. Duke University Press.

Cass, V. C. (1979). Homosexual Identity Formation: A Theoretical Model. *Journal of Homosexuality 4*(3), 219–235.

Castells, M. (2010). *The rise of the network society* (2nd ed., with a new pref). Wiley-Blackwell.

Center for Disease Control. (2018, March 23). PrEP | HIV Basics | HIV/AIDS | CDC. https://www.cdc.gov/hiv/basics/prep.html.

Chauncey, G. (1994). *Gay New York: Gender, urban culture, and the making of the gay male world, 1890–1940*. Basic Books.

Cho, S., Crenshaw, K. W., and McCall, L. (2013). Toward a Field of Intersectionality Studies: Theory, Applications, and Praxis. *Signs: Journal of Women in Culture and Society 38*(4), 785–810. https://doi.org/10.1086/669608.

Christmann, G. B. (2008). The Power of Photographs of Buildings in the Dresden Urban Discourse: Towards a Visual Discourse Analysis. *Forum: Qualitative Social Research 9*(3). http://dx.doi.org/10.17169/fqs-9.3.1163.

Christopherson, K. M. (2007). The positive and negative implications of anonymity in Internet social interactions: "On the Internet, Nobody Knows You're a Dog." *Computers in Human Behavior 23*(6), 3038–3056. https://doi.org/10.1016/j.chb.2006.09.001.

Cohen, C. J., and Jackson, S. J. (2015, December 7). Ask a Feminist: A Conversation with Cathy Cohen on Black Lives Matter, Feminism, and Contemporary Activism. *Signs: Journal of Women in Culture and Society.* http://signsjournal.org/ask-a-feminist-cohen-jackson/.

Corbin, J., and Strauss, A. (1990). Grounded theory research: Procedures, canons, and evaluative criteria. *Qualitative Sociology 13*(1).

Couldry, N. (2012). *Media, society, world: Social theory and digital media practice.* Polity.

Craig, S. L., and McInroy, L. (2014a). You Can Form a Part of Yourself Online: The Influence of New Media on Identity Development and Coming Out for LGBTQ Youth. *Journal of Gay & Lesbian Mental Health 18*(1), 95–109. https://doi.org/10.1080/19359705.2013.777007.

Crenshaw, K. (1991). Mapping the Margins: Intersectionality, Identity Politics, and Violence against Women of Color. *Stanford Law Review 43*(6), 1241. https://doi.org/10.2307/1229039.

Culler, J. D. (2011). *Literary theory: A very short introduction* (2nd ed., fully updated new ed.). Oxford University Press.

DATAGAY. (1979, May 3). *The Advocate.*

de Koff, D. (2017, August 25). Looking for a sugar daddy? Join the new dating app Daddybear—unless you're HIV-positive. *Queerty.* https://www.queerty.com/looking-sugar-daddy-join-new-dating-app-daddybear-unless-youre-hiv-positive-20170825.

de Vogue, A., and Cole, D. (2019, June 17). Supreme Court sides with Oregon bakery that refused to make cake for same-sex wedding. *CNN.* https://www.cnn.com/2019/06/17/politics/supreme-court-lgbtq-religious-liberties-oregon/index.html.

Dean, J. (2005). Communicative Capitalism: Circulation and the Foreclosure of Politics. *Cultural Politics: An International Journal 1*(1), 51–74. https://doi.org/10.2752/174321905778054845.

———. (2009). *Democracy and other neoliberal fantasies: Communicative capitalism and left politics* (Kindle Edition). Duke University Press.

Dean, T. (2008). Breeding Culture: Barebacking, Bugchasing, Giftgiving. *The Massachusetts Review 49*(1/2), 80–94. JSTOR.

D'Emilio, J. (1983). Capitalism and gay identity. In A. Snitow, C. Stansell, and S. Thompson (Eds.), *Powers of Desire: The Politics of Sexuality* (pp. 100–113). Monthly Review Press.

———. (1998). *Sexual politics, sexual communities: The making of a homosexual minority in the United States, 1940–1970* (2nd ed). University of Chicago Press.

Derrida, J. (2006). *Specters of Marx: The state of the debt, the work of mourning and the New International* (1. publ). Routledge.

Deuze, M. (2011). Media life. *Media, Culture & Society 33*(1), 137–148. https://doi.org/10.1177/0163443710386518.

DeVault, M. L., and Gross, G. (2012). Feminist Qualitative Interviewing: Experience, Talk, and Knowledge. In S. Hesse-Biber, *Handbook of Feminist Research: Theory and Praxis* (pp. 206–236). SAGE Publications. https://doi.org/10.4135/9781483384740.n11.

Dolan, M. (2019, June 14). Appeals court lets Trump's military transgender ban stand while judge reconsiders case. *LA Times.* https://www.latimes.com/local/lanow/la-me-ln-transgender-military-20190614-story.html.

Drabold, W. (2016, July 15). Here's What Mike Pence Said on LGBT Issues Over the Years. *Time.* http://time.com/4406337/mike-pence-gay-rights-lgbt-religious-freedom/.

Duggan, L. (2002). The New Homonormativity: The Sexual Politics of Neoliberalism. In R. Castronovo and D. D. Nelson (Eds.), *Materializing Democracy: Toward a Revitalized Cultural Politics* (pp. 175–194). Duke University Press. http://www.myilibrary.com?id=306409.

Eaklor, V. L. (2008). *Queer America: A GLBT history of the 20th century.* Greenwood Press.

Eisenstein, Z. (1978). *The Combahee River Collective Statement.* http://circuitous.org/scraps/combahee.html.

Etengoff, C., and Daiute, C. (2015). Online Coming-Out Communications Between Gay Men and Their Religious Family Allies: A Family of Choice and Origin Perspective. *Journal of GLBT Family Studies 11*(3), 278–304. https://doi.org/10.1080/1550428X.2014.964442.

Fitzsimons, T. (2019, July 17). GOP official says fixation with "homosexual activities" harming U.S. moral core. *NBC News.* https://www.nbcnews.com/feature/nbc-out/gop-official-says-fixation-homosexual-activities-harming-u-s-moral-n1030941.

Flick, U., Kardorff, E. von, and Steinke, I. (Eds.). (2010). *A companion to qualitative research* (repr). SAGE.

Foucault, M. (1969). *The archaeology of knowledge and, The discourse on language* (A. M. Sheridan Smith, Trans.). Vintage Books.

———. (1984). Of Other Spaces (J. Miskowiec, Trans.). *Architecture/Mouvement/Continuite,* 9.

———. (1990). *The History of Sexuality, Volume 1: An Introduction: Vol. Volume 1: An Introduction.* Vintage Books.

Frank, G. (2013). "The Civil Rights of Parents": Race and conservative politics in Anita Bryant's campaign against gay rights in 1970s Florida. *Journal of the History of Sexuality 22*(1), 126–160. https://doi.org/10.1353/sex.2013.0005.

Gertler, L. M. (2014). *The coming out experience, internatlized homophobia and self-compassion in LGBQ young adults* [Dissertation]. Wright Institute.

Gieseking, J. J., Lingel, J., and Cockayne, D. (2018). What's queer about Internet studies now? *First Monday 23*(7). https://doi.org/10.5210/fm.v23i7.9254.

Gill, R. (2000). Discourse Analysis. In M. W. Bauer and G. D. Gaskell (Eds.), *Qualitative Researching with Text, Image and Sound: A Practical Handbook for Social Research* (1st ed., pp. 172–190). SAGE Publications.

Ginelle, L. (2015, September 24). The New Stonewall Film Is Just as Whitewashed as We Feared. *Bitch Media.* https://www.bitchmedia.org/article/new-stonewall-film-just-white-washed-we-feared.

GLAAD. (2017, October 25). *Where We Are on TV Report—2017.* https://www.glaad.org/whereweareontv17.

Goodman, J. A. (2013, January 31). Preparing for a generation that comes out younger. *Huffington Post.* http://www.huffingtonpost.com/josh-a-goodman/preparing-for-a-generation-that-comes-out-younger_b_2556346.html.

Goodstein, D. B. (1980, March 6). Opening Space. *The Advocate,* 5.

Gordon, M., and Price, M. S. (2016, March 26). Understanding HB2: North Carolina's newest law solidifies state's role in defining discrimination. *Charlotte Observer.* http://www.charlotteobserver.com/news/politics-government/article68401147.html.

Gorkemli, S. (2012). "Coming out of the internet": Lesbian and gay activism and the internet as a "digital closet" in Turkey. *Journal of Middle East Women's Studies 8*(3), 63–88.

Gottfied, J., and Shearer, E. (2016, May 26). News Use Across Social Media Platforms 2016. *Pew Research Center.* http://www.journalism.org/2016/05/26/news-use-across-social-media-platforms-2016/.

Grinberg, E. (2014, September 18). Facebook "real name" policy stirs questions around identity. CNN. http://www.cnn.com/2014/09/16/living/facebook-name-policy/index.html.

Grov, C., Bimbi, D. S., Nanin, J. E., and Parsons, J. T. (2006). Race, ethnicity, gender, and generational factors associated with the coming-out process among gay, lesbian, and bisexual individuals. *The Journal of Sex Research 43*(2), 115–121.

Grov, C., Breslow, A. S., Newcomb, M. E., Rosenberger, J. G., and Bauermeister, J. A. (2014). Gay and Bisexual Men's Use of the Internet: Research from the 1990s through 2013. *The Journal of Sex Research 51*(4), 390–409. https://doi.org/10.1080/00224499.2013.871626.

Gruzd, A., Wellman, B., and Takhteyev, Y. (2011). Imagining Twitter as an Imagined Community. *American Behavioral Scientist 55*(10), 1294–1318. https://doi.org/10.1177/0002764211409378.

GSF. (1977, November 30). *The Advocate.*

———. (1979, May 3). *The Advocate.*

Gudelunas, D. (2012). There's an App for that: The Uses and Gratifications of Online Social Networks for Gay Men. *Sexuality & Culture 16*(4), 347–365. https://doi.org/10.1007/s12119-012-9127-4.

Halberstam, J. (2005). *In a queer time and place: Transgender bodies, subcultural lives.* New York University Press.

Hall, S. (1980). Encoding/decoding. In S. Hall, D. Hobson, A. Lowe, and P. Willis (Eds.), *Culture, media, language: Working papers in cultural studies, 1972–79* (Transf. to digit. print, pp. 128–138). Hutchinson.

———. (2000). The Whites of Their Eyes: Racist Ideologies and the Media. In P. Marris and S. Thornham (Eds.), *Media Studies: A Reader* (pp. 271–282). New York University Press.

Hallberg, L. R.-M. (2006). The "core category" of grounded theory: Making constant comparisons. *International Journal of Qualitative Studies on Health and Well-Being 1*(3), 141–148. https://doi.org/10.1080/17482620600858399.

Hanisch, C. (2000). The Personal is Political. In B. A. Crow (Ed.), *Radical feminism: A documentary reader* (pp. 113–116). New York University Press.

Hasenmueller, C. (1978). Panofsky, Iconography, and Semiotics. *The Journal of Aesthetics and Art Criticism 36*(3), 289. https://doi.org/10.2307/430439.

Henderson, L. (2013a). *Love and money: Queers, class, and cultural production.* New York University Press.

Henderson, L. (2013b). Queer Visibilities and Social Class. In *Love and Money: Queers, Class, and Cultural Production* (pp. 31–59). New York University Press.

Henry, P. (2018, January 19). Dear White Gay Men, Racism Is Not "Just a Preference." *Them.* https://www.them.us/story/racism-is-not-a-preference.

Herring, S. (2010). *Another country: Queer anti-urbanism.* New York University Press.

Hess, A. (2015). The Selfie Assemblage. *International Journal of Communication 9*, 1629–1646.

Heywood, I., Sandywell, B., and Gardiner, M. (Eds.). (2012). *The handbook of visual culture.* Berg.

HIV.gov. (2017, December 5). U.S. Statistics. https://www.hiv.gov/hiv-basics/overview/data-and-trends/statistics.

Hlavach, L., and Freivogel, W. H. (2011). Ethical Implications of Anonymous Comments Posted to Online News Stories. *Journal of Mass Media Ethics 26*(1), 21–37. https://doi.org/10.1080/08900523.2011.525190.

Holpuch, A. (2015, February 16). Facebook still suspending Native Americans over "real name" policy. *The Guardian.* http://www.theguardian.com/technology/2015/feb/16/facebook-real-name-policy-suspends-native-americans.

hooks, bell. (1992). *Black looks: Race and representation.* South End Press.

Hoover, S. M. (2006). *Religion in the media age.* Routledge.

———, and Clark, L. S. (2008). Children and Media in the Context of the Home and Family. In *The International Handbook of Children, Media and Culture* (pp. 105–120). SAGE Publications. https://doi.org/10.4135/9781848608436.n7.

Howard, J. (2001). *Men like that: A southern queer history.* University of Chicago Press.

Hughey, M. W., and Daniels, J. (2013). Racist comments at online news sites: A methodological dilemma for discourse analysis. *Media, Culture & Society 35*(3), 332–347. https://doi.org/10.1177/0163443712472089.

Human Rights Campaign. (2018). *Violence Against the Transgender Community in 2018.* Human Rights Campaign. http://www.hrc.org/resources/violence-against-the-transgender-community-in-2018/.

Isaksson, E. (1997, January). *Living with lesbian lists.* http://www.sappho.net/lesbian-lists/lll.html.

James, S. E., Herman, J. L., Rankin, S., Keisling, M., Mottet, L., and Anafi, M. (2016). *The report of the 2015 U.S. transgender survey* (p. 2002). National Center for Transgender Equality.

Jenkins, H. (2008). *Convergence culture: Where old and new media collide* (Updated and with a new afterword). New York University Press.

Johnson, C. (2017, March 28). Trump's U.S. Census proposes, immediately cuts LGBT questions. *Washington Blade: Gay News, Politics, LGBT Rights.* https://www.washingtonblade.com/2017/03/28/u-s-census-proposes-immediately-cuts-lgbt-questions/.

Johnson, D. K. (2004). *The lavender scare: The Cold War persecution of gays and lesbians in the federal government.* University of Chicago Press.

Johnson, P. M., and Holmes, K. A. (2017). Gaydar, Marriage, and Rip-Roaring Homosexuals: Discourses About Homosexuality in Dear Abby and Ann Landers Advice Columns, 1967–1982. *Journal of Homosexuality,* 1–18. https://doi.org/10.1080/00918369.2017.1413274.

Jones, A. (2009). Queer heterotopias: Homonormativity and the future of queerness. *A Journal of Queer Studies 4.* http://www.interalia.org.pl/en/artykuly/2009_4/13_queer_heterotopias_homonormativity_and_the_future_of_queerness.htm.

Jotanovic, D. (2017, October 25). Queering Our Cult: Why Gay Men Need To Cut Off Misogyny Now More Than Ever. *Huffington Post.* https://www.huffingtonpost.com/entry/queering-our-cult-why-gay-men-need-to-shake-off-misogyny_us_59efccd2e4b04809c050120a.

Juris, J. S. (2012). Reflections on #Occupy Everywhere: Social media, public space, and emerging logics of aggregation: Reflections on #Occupy Everywhere. *American Ethnologist 39*(2), 259–279. https://doi.org/10.1111/j.1548–1425.2012.01362.x.

Kann, L., O'Malley Olsen, E., McManus, T., Harris, W. A., Shanklin, S. L., Flint, K. H., Queen, B., Lowry, Ri., Chyen, D., Whittle, L., Thornton, J., Lim, C., Yamakawa, Y., Brener, N., and Zaza, S. (2016). *Sexual Identity, Sex of Sexual Contacts, and Health-Risk Behaviors Among Students in Grades 9–12—Youth Risk Behavior Surveillance, Selected Sites, United States, 2001–2009* (Surveillance Summaries). Centers for Disease Control. https://www.cdc.gov/mmwr/preview/mmwrhtml/ss6007a1.htm.

Karlik, M. (2019, November 11). Colorado's diversity rises—Slightly—According to census data. *Colorado Politics.* https://www.coloradopolitics.com/news/colorado-s-diversity-rises-slightly-according-to-census-data/article_48a13d2a-04be-11ea-9f45-8b293e24bc9f.html.

Kearney, M. C. (Ed.). (2011). Branding the post-feminist self: Girls' video production and YouTube. In *Mediated girlhoods: New explorations of girls' media culture* (pp. 277–294). Peter Lang.

Kellaway, M. (2015, March 14). Trans Folks Respond to "Bathroom Bills" With #WeJustNeedtoPee Selfies. *The Advocate.* http://www.advocate.com/politics/transgender/2015/03/14/trans-folks-respond-bathroom-bills-wejustneedtopee-selfies.

Knoblauch, H., Baer, A., Laurier, E., Petschke, S., and Schnettler, B. (2008). Visual Analysis. New Developments in the Interpretative Analysis of Video and Photography. *Forum: Qualitative Social Research 9*(3). https://doi.org/10.17169/fqs-9.3.1170.

Lawson, R. (2015, December 1). The Reagan Administration's Unearthed Response to the AIDS Crisis Is Chilling. *Vanity Fair.* https://www.vanityfair.com/news/2015/11/reagan-administration-response-to-aids-crisis.

Leavell, J. (2018, January 10). When Toxic Masculinity Infects Our Queer Spaces, We All Lose. *Vice.* https://www.vice.com/en_us/article/ev55y4/when-toxic-masculinity-infects-our-queer-spaces-we-all-lose.

Leppänen, S., Møller, J. S., Nørreby, T. R., Stæhr, A., and Kytölä, S. (2015). Authenticity, normativity and social media. *Discourse, Context & Media 8,* 1–5. https://doi.org/10.1016/j.dcm.2015.05.008.

LGBT Rights Milestones Fast Facts. (2016, December 26). *CNN.* http://www.cnn.com/2015/06/19/us/lgbt-rights-milestones-fast-facts/index.html.

Lim, J. S., Nicholson, J., Yang, S.-U., and Kim, H.-K. (2015). Online authenticity, popularity, and the "Real Me" in a microblogging environment. *Computers in Human Behavior 52,* 132–143. https://doi.org/10.1016/j.chb.2015.05.037.

Lindlof, T. R. (2011). *Qualitative communication research methods* (3rd ed). SAGE.

Lingel, J. (2017). *Digital countercultures and the struggle for community.* MIT Press.

Lofton, K. (2017). *Consuming religion.* University of Chicago Press.

Madrigal, N. J. and A. C. (2011, January 12). The Rise and Fall of MySpace. *The Atlantic*. https://www.theatlantic.com/technology/archive/2011/01/the-rise-and-fall-of-myspace/69444/.

mallow610. (2012, February 23). *Coming Out—Live*. https://www.youtube.com/watch?v=GESBUlXBCvE.

Manning, J. (2015). Communicating Sexual Identities: A Typology of Coming Out. *Sexuality & Culture 19*(1), 122–138. https://doi.org/10.1007/s12119–014–9251–4.

Marciano, A. (2011). The Role of Internet Newsgroups in the Coming-Out Process of Gay Male Youth: An Israeli Case Study. In E. Dunkels, G.-M. Franberg, and C. Hallgren (Eds.), *Youth Culture and Net Culture: Online Social Practices* (pp. 222–241). IGI Global. http://services.igi-global.com/resolvedoi/resolve.aspx?doi=10.4018/978–1-60960–209–3.

Marwick, A. E., and boyd, d. (2011). I tweet honestly, I tweet passionately: Twitter users, context collapse, and the imagined audience. *New Media & Society 13*(1), 114–133. https://doi.org/10.1177/1461444810365313.

Mathews, H. (2015, September 21). 25 Best "Gay Dating" Apps (Homosexual, Bi, Trans & Curious). *DatingAdvice.com*. http://www.datingadvice.com/online-dating/best-gay-dating-apps

McFarland, M. (2014, February 6). Why Mark Zuckerberg has calmed down about openness and authenticity. *Washington Post*. http://www.washingtonpost.com/blogs/innovations/wp/2014/02/06/why-mark-zuckerberg-has-calmed-down-about-openness-and-authenticity/.

McGlotten, S. (2013). *Virtual intimacies: Media, affect, and queer sociality*. State University of New York Press.

McLean, K. (2008). 'Coming Out, Again': Boundaries, identities and spaces of belonging. *Australian Geographer 39*(3), 303–313. https://doi.org/10.1080/00049180802270507.

McLuhan, M. (1994). *Understanding media: The extensions of man* (1st MIT Press ed.). MIT Press.

Meeker, M. (2006). *Contacts desired: Gay and lesbian communications and community, 1940s-1970s*. University of Chicago Press.

Mills, C. W. (1972). The Cultural Apparatus. In *Power, politics and people: The collected essays of C. Wright Mills* (Reprint, pp. 405–422). Oxford University Press.

Mohr, J. J., and Rochlen, A., B. (1999). Measuring attitudes regarding bisexuality in lesbian, gay male, and heterosexual populations. *Journal of Counseling Psychology 46*(3), 353–369.

Moore, M. J., Nakano, T., Enomoto, A., and Suda, T. (2012). Anonymity and roles associated with aggressive posts in an online forum. *Computers in Human Behavior 28*(3), 861–867. https://doi.org/10.1016/j.chb.2011.12.005.

Muñoz, J. E. (1999). *Disidentifications: Queers of color and the performance of politics*. University of Minnesota Press.

———. (2009). *Cruising utopia: The then and there of queer futurity*. New York University Press.

Name withheld. (1978, February 8). Misogyny? *The Advocate*, 3.

Nash, J. C. (2008). Re-thinking intersectionality. *Feminist Review 89*(1), 1–15. https://doi.org/10.1057/fr.2008.4.

National Conference of State Legislatures. (2017, July 28). *"Bathroom Bill" Legislative Tracking*. http://www.ncsl.org/research/education/-bathroom-bill-legislative-tracking635951130.aspx.

Ng, E. (2013). A "Post-Gay" Era? Media Gaystreaming, Homonormativity, and the Politics of LGBT Integration: A "Post-Gay" Era? Media Gaystreaming. *Communication, Culture & Critique 6*(2), 258–283. https://doi.org/10.1111/cccr.12013.

Norman, J. (2015, July 15). Goodbye to all the gay bars. Are dating apps killing queer culture? *The Guardian*. http://www.theguardian.com/commentisfree/2015/jul/15/goodbye-to-all-the-gay-bars-are-dating-apps-killing-queer-culture.

O'Hara, M. E. (2017, March 29). LGBTQ Americans will not be counted in the 2020 U.S. Census after all. *NBC News*. https://www.nbcnews.com/feature/nbc-out/lgbtq-americans-won-t-be-counted-2020-u-s-census-n739911.

Ohlheiser, A. (2014, September 4). Young gay man disowned by family in viral video receives nearly $100,000 from supporters. *Washington Post*. https://www.washingtonpost.com/news/

the-intersect/wp/2014/09/04/young-gay-man-disowned-by-family-in-viral-video-receives-nearly-100000-from-supporters/.

Omi, M., and Winant, H. (2015). *Racial formation in the United States* (Third edition). Routledge/Taylor & Francis Group.

O'Riordan, K., and Phillips, D. J. (Eds.). (2007). *Queer online: Media technology & sexuality*. Peter Lang.

O'Sullivan, S. E. M. (2017). Frontiersmen Are the "Real Men" in Trump's America: Hegemonic Masculinity at Work on U.S. Cable's Version of Blue-Collar Reality [Dissertation]. University of Colorado, Boulder.

Ott, B. L., and Mack, R. L. (2014). *Critical media studies: An introduction* (Second edition). Wiley Blackwell.

Owens, Z. D. (2015). The social meanings of sexual identity formation: Identity management, experiences of homophobia, and changing patterns of interaction among college-aged gay men [Dissertation]. University of Colorado.

Padva, G. (2008). Media and Popular Culture Representations of LGBT Bullying. *Journal of Gay & Lesbian Social Services* *19*(3–4), 105–118. https://doi.org/10.1080/10538720802161615.

Panofsky, E. (1972). *Studies in iconology: Humanistic themes in the art of the Renaissance* (Paperback ed). Westview Press.

Pew Research Center. (2013, June 13). A Survey of LGBT Americans. Pew Research Center's Social & Demographic Trends Project. http://www.pewsocialtrends.org/2013/06/13/a-survey-of-lgbt-americans/.

———. (2014, June). Political Polarization in the American Public. *Pew Research Center for the People and the Press*. http://www.people-press.org/2014/06/12/political-polarization-in-the-american-public/.

Poole, E. (2013). Hey girls, did you know? Slut-shaming on the internet needs to stop. *HeinOnline*, 45.

Puar, J. K. (2012). Coda: The Cost of Getting Better: Suicide, Sensation, Switchpoints. *GLQ: A Journal of Lesbian and Gay Studies* *18*(1), 149–158. https://doi.org/10.1215/10642684–1422179.

———. (2007). *Terrorist assemblages: Homonationalism in queer times*. Duke University Press.

———. (2010, November 16). In the wake of It Gets Better. *The Guardian*. https://www.theguardian.com/commentisfree/cifamerica/2010/nov/16/wake-it-gets-better-campaign.

———. (2012). "I would rather be a cyborg than a goddess": Becoming-Intersectional in Assemblage Theory. *Philosophia 2*(1), 49–66.

Pullen, C., and Cooper, M. (Eds.). (2010). *LGBT identity and online new media*. Routledge.

Race, K. (2015). 'Party and Play': Online hook-up devices and the emergence of PNP practices among gay men. *Sexualities 18*(3), 253–275. https://doi.org/10.1177/1363460714550913.

Ramirez, A. (2015, September 29). "Stonewall" continues Hollywood's tradition of LgbT Whitewasing. *Complex*. http://www.complex.com/pop-culture/2015/09/stonewall-lgbt-history.

Reddick, R. L. (2012). Sexual encounters: Gay male college students' use of the Internet and socia media [Dissertaton]. Iowa State University.

Redding, R. E. (2008). It's Really About Sex: Same-Sex Marriage, Lesbigay Parenting, and the Psychology of Disgust. *Duke Journal of Gender Law & Policy 15*(127), 127–193.

Reichert, T., and Lambiase, J. (Eds.). (2003). *Sex in advertising: Perspectives on the erotic appeal*. Lawrence Erlbaum Associates.

Reinecke, L., and Trepte, S. (2014). Authenticity and well-being on social network sites: A two-wave longitudinal study on the effects of online authenticity and the positivity bias in SNS communication. *Computers in Human Behavior 30*, 95–102. https://doi.org/10.1016/j.chb.2013.07.030.

Remafedi, G., Farrow, J., A., and Deisher, R., W. (1991). Risk Factors for Attempted Suicide in Gay and Bisexual Youth. *Pediatrics*.

Robertson, M. A., and Sgoutas, A. (2012). Thinking beyond the Category of Sexual Identity: At the Intersection of Sexuality and Human-Trafficking Policy. *Politics & Gender 8*(03), 421–429. https://doi.org/10.1017/S1743923X12000414.

Robinson, F. A. (n.d.). *AIDS Awareness Cards, 1993*. National Museum of American History.

Rodriguez, M. (2016, October 5). Grindr's tone-deaf undocumented immigrant tweet highlights pervading racism within the gay community. *Mic.* https://mic.com/articles/155881/grindr-s-tone-deaf-undocumented-immigrant-tweet-highlights-racism-in-the-gay-community.

———. (2017, August 21). New App For Sugar Babies is Promoting Stigma. *INTO.* https://intomore.com/impact/new-app-for-sugar-babies-is-promoting-stigma/37c0e08a93994550.

Rose, G. (2012). *Visual methodologies: An introduction to researching with visual materials* (3rd ed). SAGE.

Rosenberg, D. (2015, April 12). The Secret History of Hunky Male Beefcakes. *Slate.* http://www.slate.com/blogs/behold/2015/04/12/_100_rare_all_natural_beefcake_a_look_at_the_history_of_beefcake_photography.html.

Ross, M. B. (2005). Beyond the closet as raceless paradigm. In *Black Queer Studies: A Critical Anthology* (pp. 160–188). Duke University Press.

Rulli, M. (2017, February 22). New Study Suggests PrEP is Reducing Chlamydia & Gonorrhea By Up to 40%. *Out.* http://www.out.com/news-opinion/2017/2/22/new-study-suggests-prep-reducing-chlamydia-gonorrhea-40.

Russo, V. (1987). *The celluloid closet: Homosexuality in the movies* (Rev. ed). Harper & Row.

Saldaña, J. (2013). *The coding manual for qualitative researchers* (2nd ed). SAGE.

Sampson, T. D. (2012). *Virality: Contagion theory in the age of networks*. University of Minnesota Press.

Samuelson-Cramp, F., and Bolat, E. (2018). Helping the World One "Like" at a Time: The Rise of the Slacktivist. In G. Grigore, A. Stancu, and D. McQueen (Eds.), *Corporate Responsibility and Digital Communities: An International Perspective towards Sustainability* (pp. 123–143). Springer International Publishing. https://doi.org/10.1007/978-3-319–63480-7_7.

Santayana, G. (1982). *The life of reason. 1: Reason in common sense* (Reprint). Dover Publications.

Savage, D., and Miller, T. (2012). *It gets better: Coming out, overcoming bullying, and creating a life worth living*. Plume.

Scheufele, D. A. (1999). Framing as a Theory of Media Effects. *Journal of Communication*, 103–122.

Sears, David. O., and Freedman, J. L. (1997). Selective Exposure to Information: A Critical Review. *The Public Opinion Quarterly 31*(2), 124–213.

Sevits, K. (2018, October 1). Denver named 5th fastest-growing big city in US; Loveland, Greeley among fastest-growing overall. *The Denver Channel.* https://www.thedenverchannel.com/news/our-colorado/denver-named-5th-fastest-growing-big-city-in-us-loveland-greeley-among-fastest-growing-overall.

Shaw, A. (2015). *Gaming at the edge: Sexuality and gender at the margins of gamer culture*. University of Minnesota Press.

Shaw, A., and Sender, K. (2016). Queer technologies: Affordances, affect, ambivalence. *Critical Studies in Media Communication 33*(1), 1–5. https://doi.org/10.1080/15295036.2015.1129429

Shilts, R. (2008). *The mayor of Castro Street: The life & times of Harvey Milk*. St. Martin's Griffin.

Smith, A. (2017, January 12). Record shares of Americans have smartphones, home broadband. *Fact Tank: News in the Numbers.* http://www.pewresearch.org/fact-tank/2017/01/12/evolution-of-technology/.

Smith, L. T. (2012). *Decolonizing methodologies: Research and indigenous peoples* (Second edition). Zed Books.

Solomon, D., McAbee, J., Åsberg, K., and McGee, A. (2015). Coming Out and the Potential for Growth in Sexual Minorities: The Role of Social Reactions and Internalized Homonegativity. *Journal of Homosexuality* *62*(11), 1512–1538. https://doi.org/10.1080/00918369.2015.1073032.

Sontag, S. (2001). *On photography*. Picador USA.

Sorren, M. (2015, February). *Grey's Anatomy*'s Transgender Storyline Had A Lot Of Important, Teachable Moments, But 1 Big Mistake. *Bustle*. http://www.bustle.com/articles/65461-greys-anatomys-transgender-storyline-had-a-lot-of-important-teachable-moments-but-1-big-mistake.

Stewart-Winter, T. (2016). *Queer clout: Chicago and the rise of gay politics*. University of Pennsylvania Press.

Street, M. (2018, January 20). Gay Porn Stars Clash Over The Term "Big Black C*ck": Is It Ever Acceptable To Say? *NewNowNext*. http://www.newnownext.com/gay-porn-stars-clash-over-the-term-big-black-cck-is-race-play-ever-acceptable/01/2018/.

Strudwick, P. (2016, February 9). The Founders Of This Gay Dating App Won't Stop You Searching By Race. *BuzzFeed*. https://www.buzzfeed.com/patrickstrudwick/this-is-how-gay-dating-app-bosses-defend-racial-filtering.

Sue, D. W. (2010). *Microaggressions in everyday life: Race, gender, and sexual orientation* (Kindle). Wiley.

Swain, K. W. (2007, June 24). Gay pride needs new direction. *Denver Post*, E.1.

Taylor, J. (2017, April 11). Pastor who said Pulse victims got "what they deserve" was molesting young teens. *LGBTQ Nation*. https://www.lgbtqnation.com/2017/04/pastor-went-pulse-victims-guilty-molestation-charges-boy-girl/.

Teo, A. R. (2013). Social isolation associated with depression: A case report of *hikikomori*. *International Journal of Social Psychiatry* *59*(4), 339–341. https://doi.org/10.1177/0020764012437128.

Tharrett, M. (2015, August 25). Windows 10 "Privacy" Feature is Effectively Outing Young Kids to Their Parents. *NewNowNext*. http://www.newnownext.com/windows-10-privacy-feature-is-effectively-outing-young-kids-to-their-parents/08/2015/.

The Nielson Company. (2017). *Social Studies: A Look at the Social Landscape* (2016 Nielson Social Media Report). The Nielson Company. http://www.nielsen.com/content/dam/corporate/us/en/reports-downloads/2017-reports/2016-nielsen-social-media-report.pdf.

The Trevor Project. (2019). *The Trevor Project National Survey on LGBTQ Youth Mental Health 2019*. https://www.thetrevorproject.org/wp-content/uploads/2019/06/The-Trevor-Project-National-Survey-Results-2019.pdf

Thompson, E. P. (1967). Time, Work-Discipline, and Industrial Capitalism. *Past & Present 38*, 56–97.

Tönnies, F. (2002). *Community and society* (C. P. Loomis, Trans.). Dover Publications.

Trott, D. (2017, June 19). An Open Letter To Gay, White Men: No, You're Not Allowed To Have A Racial Preference. *Huffington Post*. https://www.huffingtonpost.com/entry/an-open-letter-to-gay-white-men-no-youre-not-allowed_us_5947f0ffe4b0f7875b83e459.

Tyrangiel, J. (2000, February 6). The Gay Chat Room. *Time*. http://content.time.com/time/magazine/article/0,9171,38816,00.html.

Urquhart, C., Lehmann, H., and Myers, M. D. (2009). Putting the "theory" back into grounded theory: Guidelines for grounded theory studies in information systems: Guidelines for grounded theory studies in information systems. *Information Systems Journal 20*(4), 357–381. https://doi.org/10.1111/j.1365-2575.2009.00328.x.

van Dijck, J. (2013). *The culture of connectivity: A critical history of social media*. Oxford University Press.

Village People. (1978, February). "Macho Man."

Visser, N. (2017, March 29). The U.S. Won't Tally LGBT People In 2020 Census. *Huffington Post*. https://www.huffingtonpost.com/entry/us-census-lgbt-americans_us_58db3894e4b0cb23e65c6cd9

Walker, J. (2016, July 19). Before Grindr and Scruff: A brief oral history of gay men finding each other online. *Splinter*. https://splinternews.com/before-grindr-and-scruff-a-brief-oral-history-of-gay-m-1793860384.

Wang, H. L. (2018, March 30). 2020 Census Will Ask About Same-Sex Relationships. *NPR.* https://www.npr.org/2018/03/30/598192154/2020-census-will-ask-about-same-sex-relationships.

Watson, T. (1977, November 30). Introducing *The Advocate* Experience. *The Advocate*, 7.

Wight, J. (2014). Queer Sweet Home: Disorientation, Tyranny, and Silence in Digital Space. *Cultural Studies & Critical Methodologies 14*(2), 128–137. https://doi.org/10.1177/1532708613512269.

Willenbecher, T. (1980, March 6). Quick Encounters of the Closest Kind: The Bush League— The Rites and Rituals of Shadow Sex. *The Advocate*, 16–18.

Williams, A. (2005, August 28). Do You MySpace? *The New York Times.* https://www.nytimes.com/2005/08/28/fashion/sundaystyles/do-you-myspace.html.

Wilson, M. (2015, February 28). *Facebook lets you choose a custom gender, now it's time to drop real names.* Betanews. http://betanews.com/2015/02/28/facebook-lets-you-choose-a-custom-gender-now-its-time-to-drop-real-names/.

Wilson, N. (2017, May 11). Gay people "deserve to die," SLO High teacher's letter to student newspaper says. *The Tribune.* http://www.sanluisobispo.com/news/local/education/article149885747.html.

Zane, Z. (2017, September 13). A Man on Grindr Saved Another Man from Committing Suicide. *Pride.* https://www.pride.com/lgbt/2017/9/13/man-grindr-saved-another-man-committing-suicide.

Facebook, social media privacy, and the use and abuse of data, United States Senate, SH-216 (2018) (testimony of Mark Zuckerberg). https://www.judiciary.senate.gov/meetings/facebook-social-media-privacy-and-the-use-and-abuse-of-data.

(n.d.). *Blue Notes-Flash 1*(8).

Index

About the Author

Patrick M. Johnson, PhD, is currently an assistant professor and the program coordinator for the department of communication at Indiana University Northwest. Patrick had previously served as an assistant professor in the Department of Broadcasting and Journalism at Western Illinois University. He holds a PhD in media studies/journalism and mass communication from the University of Colorado Boulder, an MA in liberal arts and sciences from San Diego State University, and a BS in television–radio from Ithaca College. Patrick has a wide range of research and teaching interests including: social media and political expression, digital activism, media and intersectionality, queer and feminist theory, critical cultural theory, video and audio production, broadcast journalism, public speaking, and more.

Made in United States
North Haven, CT
16 November 2022